PASTA*bilities*

Publications International, Ltd.

Louis Weber, CEO
Publications International, Ltd.
8140 Lehigh Ave
Morton Grove, IL 60053

Pictured on the front cover: Pasta Primavera with Ricotta *(page 159).*

Pictured on the back cover *(clockwise from top left):* Orecchiette with Sausage and Broccoli Rabe *(page 134),* Greek Noodle Salad *(page 35),* Spicy Chicken Rigatoni *(page 129),* Vegetable Beef Noodle Soup *(page 32)* and Turkey Veggie Lasagna *(page 74).*

ISBN: 978-1-63938-749-6

Manufactured in China.

8 7 6 5 4 3 2 1

Microwave Cooking: Microave ovens vary in wattage. Use the cooking times as guidelines and check for doneness before adding more time.

WARNING: Food preparation, baking and cooking involve inherent dangers: misuse of electric products, sharp electric tools, boiling water, hot stoves, allergic reactions, foodborne illnesses and the like, pose numerous potential risks. Publications International, Ltd. (PIL) assumes no responsibility or liability for any damages you may experience as a result of following recipes, instructions, tips or advice in this publication.

While we hope this publication helps you find new ways to eat delicious foods, you may not always achieve the results desired due to variations in ingredients, cooking temperatures, typos, errors, omissions or individual cooking abilities.

TABLE OF CONTENTS

SUPER SOUPS

Italian Fish Soup

- **1 cup meatless pasta sauce**
- **¾ cup water**
- **¾ cup chicken broth**
- **1 teaspoon Italian seasoning**
- **¾ cup uncooked small pasta shells**
- **4 ounces fresh halibut or haddock steak, 1 inch thick, skinned and cut into 1-inch pieces**
- **1½ cups frozen vegetable blend, such as broccoli, carrots and water chestnuts or broccoli, carrots and cauliflower**

1 Combine pasta sauce, water, broth and Italian seasoning in medium saucepan; bring to a boil over high heat. Stir in pasta; return to a boil. Reduce heat to medium-low; cover and simmer 5 minutes.

2 Stir in fish and frozen vegetables; return to a boil. Reduce heat to medium-low; cover and simmer 4 to 5 minutes or until pasta is tender and fish begins to flake when tested with fork.

Makes 2 servings

Vietnamese Beef Soup

- **4 cups water**
- **2 ounces angel hair pasta, broken in half**
- **2¼ cups beef broth**
- **1 shallot, sliced**
- **1 whole star anise**
- **½ teaspoon minced fresh ginger**
- **1 teaspoon fish sauce**
- **1 teaspoon reduced-sodium soy sauce**
- **½ teaspoon hot pepper sauce**
- **6 ounces boneless beef sirloin, cut into ⅛-inch-thick slices**
- **⅛ teaspoon salt**
- **⅛ teaspoon black pepper**
- **1 cup bean sprouts**
- **2 green onions, thinly sliced**
- **1 small fresh red chile pepper, thinly sliced**
- **2 tablespoons fresh cilantro leaves**
- **2 lime wedges**

1. Bring water to a boil in medium saucepan over medium-high heat. Add pasta; cook 3 to 4 minutes or until tender. Drain pasta; set aside.
2. Combine broth, shallot, star anise and ginger in same saucepan; bring to a boil over high heat. Reduce heat to medium-low; simmer 10 minutes. Strain broth mixture into large saucepan; stir in fish sauce, soy sauce and hot pepper sauce.
3. Season beef with salt and pepper. Add beef and bean sprouts to broth mixture; cook 1 to 2 minutes or until beef is no longer pink. Stir in cooked pasta and green onions; cook 1 minute or until heated through.
4. Top soup with chile slices and cilantro; serve with lime wedges.

Makes 2 servings

Hearty Minestrone

- 1 tablespoon olive oil
- ½ cup chopped onion
- 1 stalk celery, diced
- 1 carrot, diced
- 2 cloves garlic, minced
- 2 cups vegetable broth
- 1½ cups water
- 1 bay leaf
- ¾ teaspoon salt
- ½ teaspoon dried basil
- ½ teaspoon dried oregano
- ¼ teaspoon dried thyme
- ¼ teaspoon sugar
- ¼ teaspoon black pepper
- 1 can (about 15 ounces) dark red kidney beans, rinsed and drained
- 1 can (about 15 ounces) navy beans or cannellini beans, rinsed and drained
- 1 can (about 14 ounces) diced tomatoes
- 1 cup diced zucchini (about 1 small)
- ½ cup uncooked small pasta shells
- ½ cup frozen cut green beans
- ¼ cup dry red wine
- 1 cup packed chopped stemmed fresh spinach
- Grated Parmesan cheese (optional)

1. Heat oil in large saucepan or Dutch oven over medium-high heat. Add onion, celery, carrot and garlic; cook 5 to 7 minutes or until vegetables are tender, stirring frequently. Add broth, water, bay leaf, salt, basil, oregano, thyme, sugar and pepper; bring to a boil.
2. Stir in kidney beans, navy beans, tomatoes, zucchini, pasta, green beans and wine; cook over medium heat 10 minutes, stirring occasionally.
3. Stir in spinach; cook 2 minutes or until pasta and zucchini are tender. Remove and discard bay leaf. Serve with cheese, if desired.

Makes 4 to 6 servings

Asian Chicken Noodle Soup

- **4 dried black Chinese mushrooms**
- **2 teaspoons dry sherry**
- **1 boneless skinless chicken breast, thinly sliced**
- **8 ounces Chinese-style thin egg noodles**
- **2 cups chicken broth**
- **1 tablespoon soy sauce**
- **¼ cup sliced bamboo shoots**
- **1 small bunch watercress *or* ½ bunch stemmed fresh spinach, cut into 2-inch strips**
- **1 teaspoon dark sesame oil**
- **Dash white pepper**
- **2 green onions, thinly sliced**

1 Place mushrooms in medium bowl; add warm water to cover. Soak 20 to 40 minutes or until soft. Cut off and discard stems; cut caps into thin slices.

2 Meanwhile, drizzle sherry over chicken in medium bowl; let stand 15 minutes. Cook noodles according to package directions until tender but still firm. Drain and rinse under cool water.

3 Combine broth and soy sauce in medium saucepan; bring to a boil over high heat. Stir in mushrooms, chicken and bamboo shoots. Reduce heat to medium-low; cook 4 minutes. Add watercress, sesame oil and pepper; cook 1 minute. Add noodles; cook until heated through. Sprinkle with green onions.

Makes 2 servings

TIP To store leftover bamboo shoots, place the shoots in a jar with a tight-fitting lid and add water to cover. Store tightly sealed in the refrigerator for up to 10 days, changing the water daily.

Pasta e Fagioli

- 2 tablespoons olive oil
- 1 cup chopped onion
- 3 cloves garlic, minced
- 2 cans (about 14 ounces each) Italian-style stewed tomatoes, undrained
- 3 cups vegetable broth
- 1 can (about 15 ounces) cannellini or Great Northern beans, undrained
- ¼ cup chopped fresh Italian parsley
- 1 teaspoon dried basil
- ¼ teaspoon black pepper
- 4 ounces uncooked small pasta shells

1. Heat oil in large saucepan over medium heat. Add onion and garlic; cook 5 minutes or until onion is tender, stirring frequently.
2. Add tomatoes, broth, beans with liquid, parsley, basil and pepper; bring to a boil over high heat, stirring occasionally. Reduce heat to low; cover and simmer 10 minutes.
3. Stir in pasta; cover and cook over medium heat 10 minutes or just until pasta is tender. Serve immediately.

Makes 6 to 8 servings

Rustic Country Turkey Soup

- **1 tablespoon olive oil**
- **1 cup chopped onion**
- **¾ cup sliced carrots**
- **4 ounces sliced mushrooms**
- **1 teaspoon minced garlic**
- **2 cans (about 14 ounces each) chicken broth**
- **2 ounces uncooked rotini pasta**
- **1 teaspoon dried thyme or dried parsley flakes**
- **½ teaspoon poultry seasoning**
- **⅛ teaspoon red pepper flakes**
- **2 cups chopped cooked turkey**
- **¼ cup chopped fresh parsley**

1 Heat oil in large saucepan or Dutch oven over medium-high heat. Add onion and carrots; cook and stir 2 minutes. Add mushrooms; cook 2 minutes. Add garlic; cook and stir 30 seconds. Add broth; bring to a boil.

2 Stir in pasta, thyme, poultry seasoning and red pepper flakes; return to a boil. Reduce heat to low; cover and simmer 8 minutes or until pasta is tender.

3 Remove from heat; stir in turkey and fresh parsley. Cover and let stand 5 minutes before serving.

Makes 4 servings

Italian Wedding Soup

MEATBALLS

- 2 eggs
- 2 cloves garlic, minced
- 1 teaspoon salt
- ⅛ teaspoon black pepper
- 1½ pounds meat loaf mix (ground beef and pork)
- ¾ cup plain dry bread crumbs
- ½ cup grated Parmesan cheese
- 2 tablespoons olive oil

SOUP

- 1 onion, chopped
- 2 carrots, chopped
- 4 cloves garlic, minced
- 2 heads escarole or curly endive, coarsely chopped
- 8 cups chicken broth
- 1 can (about 14 ounces) Italian plum tomatoes, undrained, coarsely chopped
- 3 sprigs fresh thyme
- 1 teaspoon salt
- ½ teaspoon red pepper flakes
- 1 cup uncooked acini di pepe pasta

1. For meatballs, beat eggs, 2 cloves garlic, 1 teaspoon salt and black pepper in large bowl until blended. Stir in meat loaf mix, bread crumbs and cheese; mix gently until well blended. Shape mixture by tablespoonfuls into 1-inch balls.
2. Heat oil in large saucepan or Dutch oven over medium heat. Cook meatballs in batches 5 minutes or until browned. Remove to plate; set aside.
3. For soup, add onion, carrots and 4 cloves garlic to same saucepan; cook and stir 5 minutes or until onion is lightly browned. Add escarole; cook and stir 2 minutes or until wilted. Stir in broth, tomatoes with juice, thyme, 1 teaspoon salt and red pepper flakes; bring to a boil over high heat. Reduce heat to medium-low; cook 15 minutes, stirring occasionally.
4. Add meatballs and pasta to soup; return to a boil over high heat. Reduce heat to medium; cook 10 minutes or until pasta is tender. Remove and discard thyme sprigs.

Makes 8 servings

Japanese-Style Noodle Soup

- 1 package (8½ ounces) Japanese udon noodles
- 1 tablespoon vegetable oil
- 1 medium red bell pepper, cut into thin strips
- 1 medium carrot, diagonally sliced
- 2 green onions, thinly sliced
- 2 cans (about 14 ounces each) beef broth
- 1 cup water
- 1 teaspoon reduced-sodium soy sauce
- ½ teaspoon grated fresh ginger
- ½ teaspoon black pepper
- 2 cups thinly sliced fresh shiitake mushrooms, stems discarded
- 4 ounces daikon (Japanese radish), peeled and cut into thin strips
- 4 ounces firm tofu, drained and cut into ½-inch cubes

1. Cook noodles according to package directions. Drain and rinse noodles; set aside.
2. Heat oil in large saucepan over medium-high heat. Add bell pepper, carrot and green onions; cook and stir 3 minutes or until vegetables are slightly softened.
3. Stir in broth, water, soy sauce, ginger and black pepper; bring to a boil. Stir in mushrooms, daikon and tofu. Reduce heat to low; cook 5 minutes.
4. Place noodles in serving bowls; ladle soup over noodles.

Makes 6 servings

Pasta e Ceci

- **4 tablespoons olive oil, divided**
- **1 onion, chopped**
- **1 carrot, chopped**
- **1 clove garlic, minced**
- **1 sprig fresh rosemary**
- **1 teaspoon salt**
- **1 can (28 ounces) whole tomatoes, drained and crushed (see Tip)**
- **2 cups vegetable broth**
- **1 can (about 15 ounces) chickpeas, undrained**
- **1 bay leaf**
- **⅛ teaspoon red pepper flakes**
- **1 cup uncooked orecchiette pasta**
- **Black pepper (optional)**
- **Chopped fresh parsley or basil (optional)**

1. Heat 3 tablespoons oil in large saucepan over medium-high heat. Add onion and carrot; cook 10 minutes or until vegetables are soft, stirring occasionally.
2. Add garlic, rosemary and salt; cook and stir 1 minute. Stir in tomatoes, broth, chickpeas with liquid, bay leaf and red pepper flakes. Remove 1 cup mixture to food processor or blender; process until smooth. Stir puréed mixture back into saucepan; bring to a boil.
3. Stir in pasta. Reduce heat to medium; cook 12 to 15 minutes or until pasta is tender and soup is creamy. Remove and discard bay leaf and rosemary sprig. Taste and season with additional salt and black pepper, if desired. Garnish with parsley; drizzle with remaining 1 tablespoon oil.

Makes 4 servings

TIP To crush the tomatoes, take them out of the can one at a time and crush them between your fingers over the pot. Or coarsely chop them with a knife.

Spinach Ginger Noodle Soup

- **6 cups chicken broth**
- **4 ounces uncooked vermicelli pasta, broken into thirds**
- **1½ cups matchstick carrots**
- **3 ounces fresh snow peas, cut into halves**
- **4 cups packed stemmed fresh spinach (4 ounces)**
- **1½ cups cooked shrimp or chicken**
- **½ cup finely chopped green onions**
- **1 tablespoon grated fresh ginger**
- **1 teaspoon soy sauce**
- **⅛ to ¼ teaspoon red pepper flakes**

1. Heat broth to a boil in large saucepan or Dutch oven over high heat. Add pasta; return to a boil. Cook until al dente (about 2 minutes less than package directions).
2. Stir in carrots and snow peas; cook 2 minutes or until pasta is tender.
3. Remove from heat; stir in spinach, shrimp, green onions, ginger, soy sauce and red pepper flakes. Cover and let stand 2 minutes before serving.

Makes 4 servings

Pasta and Bean Soup

- 1¼ cups dried navy beans
- 6 cups cold water
- 3 slices bacon, finely chopped
- 1 onion, chopped
- 1 stalk celery, chopped
- 12 ounces smoked pork rib or neck bones
- 2 cloves garlic, minced
- ½ teaspoon dried thyme
- ½ teaspoon dried marjoram
- ¼ teaspoon black pepper
- ¾ cup uncooked small pasta shells
- 2 tablespoons chopped fresh parsley
- Salt
- 1 cup beef broth (optional)
- Grated Parmesan cheese

1. Rinse beans well in colander under cold running water, picking out any debris or blemished beans. Combine beans and water in large saucepan. To quick soak beans, bring to a boil over high heat; boil 2 minutes. Remove from heat; cover and let stand 1 hour. Do not drain.
2. Cook bacon in medium skillet over medium-high heat 2 minutes. Add onion and celery; cook and stir 6 minutes or until golden brown. Remove mixture to plate; drain off drippings.
3. Add pork bones to saucepan with beans and soaking water. Stir in bacon mixture, garlic, thyme, marjoram and pepper; bring to a boil over high heat. Reduce heat to medium-low; cook 1 hour or until beans are tender, stirring occasionally. Remove from heat.
4. Remove pork bones to plate; set aside to cool. Transfer half of bean mixture to food processor or blender with slotted spoon. Add 2 tablespoons liquid from soup; process until smooth.
5. Stir pureéd bean mixture back into soup; bring to a boil over high heat. Stir in pasta. Reduce heat to medium-low; cook 10 minutes or until pasta is tender, stirring occasionally.
6. Meanwhile, remove meat from bones; discard bones. Chop pork into bite-size pieces. Stir pork and parsley into soup; season with salt. If soup is too thick, add broth until desired consistency is reached. Sprinkle with cheese.

Makes 6 servings

Sausage Vegetable Rotini Soup

- **1 tablespoon olive oil**
- **6 ounces bulk pork sausage**
- **1 cup chopped onion**
- **1 cup chopped green bell pepper**
- **3 cups beef broth**
- **1 can (about 14 ounces) diced tomatoes**
- **¼ cup ketchup**
- **2 teaspoons chili powder**
- **½ teaspoon salt**
- **4 ounces uncooked tri-colored rotini pasta**
- **1 cup frozen corn, thawed and drained**

1. Heat oil in large saucepan over medium-high heat. Add sausage; cook 3 minutes or until no longer pink, stirring to break up sausage. Drain fat.
2. Add onion and bell pepper to saucepan; cook and stir 3 to 4 minutes or until onion is translucent.
3. Add broth, tomatoes, ketchup, chili powder and salt; bring to a boil over high heat. Stir in pasta; return to a boil. Reduce heat to medium-low; cook, uncovered, 12 minutes.
4. Stir in corn; cook 2 minutes or until pasta is tender and corn is heated through.

Makes 4 servings

One-Pot Chinese Chicken Soup

6 cups chicken broth
2 cups water
1 pound boneless skinless chicken thighs
⅓ cup reduced-sodium soy sauce
1 package (16 ounces) frozen stir-fry vegetables
6 ounces uncooked dried thin Chinese egg noodles
1 to 3 tablespoons sriracha sauce

1 Combine broth, water, chicken and soy sauce in medium saucepan; bring to a boil over high heat. Reduce heat to low; cover and simmer 20 minutes or until chicken is cooked through and very tender. Remove chicken to plate; let stand until cool enough to handle.

2 Meanwhile, add vegetables and noodles to broth in saucepan; bring to a boil over high heat. Reduce heat to medium-high; cook 5 minutes or until noodles are tender and vegetables are heated through, stirring occasionally.

3 Shred chicken into bite-size pieces. Stir chicken and 1 tablespoon sriracha into soup; taste and add additional sriracha for a spicier flavor.

Makes 4 servings

Italian Fennel Pasta Soup

1 tablespoon olive oil
1 small fennel bulb, trimmed and chopped into ¼-inch pieces (1½ cups)
4 cloves garlic, minced
3 cups vegetable broth
1 cup uncooked small pasta shells
1 teaspoon salt
1 medium zucchini or yellow squash, cut into ½-inch pieces
1 can (about 14 ounces) Italian-style diced tomatoes
¼ cup grated Romano or Parmesan cheese
¼ cup chopped fresh basil
Dash black pepper (optional)

1 Heat oil in large saucepan over medium heat. Add fennel; cook and stir 5 minutes. Add garlic; cook and stir 30 seconds. Add broth, pasta and salt; bring to a boil over high heat. Reduce heat to low; cook 5 minutes.

2 Stir in zucchini; cook 5 to 7 minutes or until pasta and vegetables are tender.

3 Stir in tomatoes; cook until heated through. Top with cheese, basil and pepper, if desired.

Makes 6 servings

Vegetable Beef Noodle Soup

- **1 tablespoon olive oil**
- **8 ounces beef for stew (½-inch pieces)**
- **¾ cup unpeeled cubed potato (1 medium)**
- **½ cup sliced carrot**
- **1 tablespoon balsamic vinegar**
- **¾ teaspoon dried thyme**
- **¼ teaspoon black pepper**
- **2½ cups beef broth**
- **1 cup water**
- **¼ cup chili sauce or ketchup**
- **2 ounces uncooked thin egg noodles**
- **¾ cup jarred or canned pearl onions, rinsed and drained**
- **¼ cup frozen peas**

1 Heat oil in large saucepan over medium-high heat. Add beef; cook 6 minutes or until browned on all sides, stirring occasionally. Remove to plate.

2 Add potato, carrot, vinegar, thyme and pepper to saucepan; cook over medium heat 3 minutes, scraping up browned bits from bottom of saucepan. Add broth, water and chili sauce; bring to a boil over medium-high heat. Stir in beef. Reduce heat to medium-low; cover and simmer 30 minutes or until beef is almost fork-tender.

3 Return to a boil over medium-high heat. Add noodles; cover and cook 7 to 10 minutes or until noodles are tender, stirring occasionally. Add onions and peas; cook 1 minute or until heated through. Serve immediately.

Makes 6 servings

PASTA SALAD

Greek Noodle Salad

2 packages (3 ounces each) ramen noodles, broken in half*
3 tablespoons extra virgin olive oil
Juice of 1 lemon
2 tablespoons red wine vinegar
1 teaspoon dried oregano
1 cup grape tomatoes, halved
¾ cup diced cucumber
½ cup crumbled feta cheese
¼ cup Kalamata olives, slivered
2 tablespoons chopped fresh parsley

***Use any flavor; discard seasoning packets.**

1 Cook noodles according to package directions; drain and rinse under cold water.

2 Whisk oil, lemon juice, vinegar and oregano in large bowl until well blended.

3 Add noodles, tomatoes, cucumber, cheese, olives and parsley; toss to coat.

Makes 4 servings

Lentil and Orzo Salad

- 8 cups water
- ½ cup dried lentils, rinsed and sorted
- 4 ounces uncooked orzo pasta
- 1½ cups quartered cherry tomatoes
- ¾ cup finely chopped celery
- ½ cup chopped red onion
- 2 ounces pitted olives (about 16 olives), coarsely chopped
- 3 to 4 tablespoons cider vinegar
- 1 tablespoon olive oil
- 2 teaspoons dried basil
- 1 clove garlic, minced
- ⅛ teaspoon red pepper flakes
- 4 ounces crumbled feta cheese with sun-dried tomatoes and basil

1. Bring water to a boil in large saucepan over high heat. Add lentils; cook 12 minutes.
2. Add orzo; cook 10 minutes or just until tender. Drain and rinse under cold water to cool completely. Drain well.
3. Meanwhile, combine tomatoes, celery, onion, olives, vinegar, oil, basil, garlic and red pepper flakes in large bowl; mix well.
4. Add lentil mixture to tomato mixture; stir gently to blend. Gently stir in cheese. Let stand 15 minutes before serving.

Makes 4 servings

Green Bean Blue Cheese Pasta Salad

- 2 cups uncooked gemelli pasta
- 2 cups trimmed halved green beans
- 3 tablespoons olive oil
- 2 tablespoons white wine vinegar
- 1 tablespoon chopped fresh thyme
- 1 tablespoon Dijon mustard
- 1 tablespoon lemon juice
- 1 teaspoon honey
- ½ teaspoon salt
- ¼ teaspoon black pepper
- ½ cup chopped walnuts, toasted*
- ½ cup crumbled blue cheese

**To toast walnuts, cook in small skillet over medium heat 1 to 2 minutes or until lightly browned, stirring frequently.*

1 Cook pasta according to package directions, adding beans during last 4 minutes of cooking. Drain pasta and beans; transfer to large bowl.

2 Meanwhile, whisk oil, vinegar, thyme, mustard, lemon juice, honey, salt and pepper in small bowl until well blended.

3 Pour dressing over pasta and green beans; toss to coat. Gently stir in walnuts and cheese. Serve warm or cover and refrigerate until ready to serve.**

***If serving cold, stir walnuts into salad just before serving.*

Makes 8 servings

Peanut Noodle and Edamame Salad

- ½ (8-ounce) package brown rice pad thai noodles
- 3 tablespoons soy sauce
- 2 tablespoons dark sesame oil
- 2 tablespoons unseasoned rice vinegar
- 1 tablespoon sugar
- 1 tablespoon finely grated fresh ginger
- 1 tablespoon creamy peanut butter
- 1 tablespoon sriracha or hot chili sauce
- 2 teaspoons minced garlic
- ½ cup thawed frozen shelled edamame
- ¼ cup shredded carrots
- ¼ cup sliced green onions
- Chopped peanuts (optional)

1. Prepare noodles according to package directions for pasta. Drain and rinse under cold water. Cut noodles into 3-inch lengths; place in large bowl.
2. Whisk soy sauce, oil, vinegar, sugar, ginger, peanut butter, sriracha and garlic in small bowl until smooth and well blended.
3. Pour dressing over noodles; toss gently to coat. Stir in edamame and carrots. Cover and refrigerate at least 30 minutes before serving. Top with green onions and peanuts, if desired.

Makes 4 servings

NOTE Brown rice pad thai noodles can be found in the Asian section of the supermarket. Regular thin rice noodles or whole wheat spaghetti may be substituted.

Quick Niçoise Pasta Salad

- **12 ounces uncooked rotini pasta**
- **1 bottle (8 ounces) Italian vinaigrette, divided**
- **1 can (about 6 ounces) tuna packed in water, drained**
- **3 hard-cooked eggs, peeled and cut into wedges**
- **1 cup frozen green beans, thawed**
- **¼ cup pitted black olives**

1. Cook pasta according to package directions; drain and transfer to large bowl.
2. Reserve ¼ cup vinaigrette. Pour remaining vinaigrette over pasta; toss to coat. Place on serving platter or individual plates.
3. Arrange tuna, eggs, green beans and olives over pasta; drizzle with reserved vinaigrette. Serve chilled or at room temperature.

Makes 6 servings

Pasta Waldorf

- 8 ounces uncooked small pasta shells
- 2 Red Delicious apples, peeled and diced
- 1 stalk celery, chopped
- ½ cup chopped pecans
- ½ cup chopped raisins
- ⅓ cup lemon yogurt
- ⅓ cup mayonnaise
- ¼ teaspoon salt

1. Cook pasta according to package directions; drain and rinse under cold water.
2. Combine pasta, apples, celery, pecans, raisins, yogurt, mayonnaise and salt in large bowl; toss to coat. Cover and refrigerate 10 minutes before serving.

Makes 6 servings

Orzo, Black Bean and Edamame Salad

- ⅔ cup uncooked orzo pasta
- ¾ cup frozen shelled edamame
- ¾ cup diced carrots
- ¾ cup canned black beans, rinsed and drained
- ½ cup diced green bell pepper
- 3 tablespoons lime juice
- 2 tablespoons olive oil
- ½ teaspoon salt
- ⅛ teaspoon black pepper
- 2 tablespoons finely chopped fresh cilantro
- 2 tablespoons grated Parmesan cheese

1 Cook orzo in medium saucepan of boiling salted water until tender, adding edamame and carrots during last 5 minutes of cooking. Drain and transfer to large bowl; stir in black beans and bell pepper.

2 Whisk lime juice, oil, salt and black pepper in small bowl until well blended. Pour dressing over salad. Sprinkle with cilantro and cheese; toss gently to coat. Serve lukewarm or at room temperature.

Makes 4 servings

Grilled Tuna, Fennel and Pasta Salad

- 8 ounces small pasta shells, cooked and drained
- Balsamic Vinaigrette (recipe follows)
- 12 ounces tuna steaks
- 2 teaspoons Dijon mustard
- 4 cups torn red leaf lettuce
- 2 cups sliced asparagus, cooked until crisp-tender and cooled
- ½ cup thinly sliced fennel bulb
- ½ cup thinly sliced red bell pepper
- 8 cherry tomatoes, halved
- Salt and black pepper

1. Cook pasta according to package directions; drain and rinse under cold water.
2. Meanwhile, oil grid. Prepare grill for direct cooking over medium-high heat or preheat broiler. Prepare Balsamic Vinaigrette.
3. Brush sides of tuna with mustard. Grill tuna or broil 6 inches from heat source about 5 minutes per side or until fish begins to flake when tested with fork. Remove to plate; break into chunks.
4. Combine tuna, pasta, lettuce, asparagus, fennel, bell pepper and tomatoes in large bowl. Drizzle with dressing; toss gently to coat. Season with salt and black pepper.

Makes 4 servings

Balsamic Vinaigrette

- ¼ cup water
- ¼ cup balsamic vinegar
- 3 tablespoons olive oil
- 2 tablespoons minced red or green onion
- 3 cloves garlic, minced
- ¾ teaspoon dried chervil
- ½ teaspoon celery seeds
- ¼ teaspoon salt
- ⅛ teaspoon black pepper

Combine all ingredients in jar with tight-fitting lid; shake until well blended. Refrigerate until ready to use. Shake again before using.

Makes about ⅔ cup

Tahini Lentil Ramen Salad

- **1 cup dried lentils, rinsed and sorted**
- **1 cup small broccoli florets**
- **1 package (3 ounces) ramen noodles***
- **3 tablespoons olive oil**
- **1 tablespoon tahini**
- **Juice of 1 lemon**
- **1 teaspoon salt**
- **⅛ teaspoon red pepper flakes**
- **1 medium tomato, diced**

****Use any flavor; discard seasoning packet.***

1. Bring 6 cups water to a boil in medium saucepan over medium-high heat. Stir in lentils. Reduce heat to medium-low; cover and cook 35 minutes.
2. Stir in broccoli; cook 2 minutes. Stir in noodles; cook 2 minutes. Drain well.
3. Whisk oil, tahini, lemon juice, salt and red pepper flakes in large bowl until well blended.
4. Add lentil-noodle mixture and tomato to dressing; toss to coat. Refrigerate 20 minutes before serving.

Makes 4 servings

Shrimp and Soba Noodle Salad

- 4 ounces soba noodles
- 1 tablespoon vegetable oil
- 2 cups diagonally sliced green beans (bite-size pieces)
- 1½ cups sliced mushrooms
- 2 tablespoons orange juice
- 2 tablespoons lime juice
- 1 tablespoon soy sauce
- 2 teaspoons dark sesame oil
- 1½ cups (6 ounces) cooked medium shrimp
- ¼ cup thinly sliced red bell pepper
- 2 tablespoons finely chopped fresh cilantro
- 1 to 2 tablespoons toasted sesame seeds (optional)

1. Cook noodles according to package directions; drain and rinse under warm water. Transfer to large bowl.
2. Heat oil in large skillet over medium-high heat. Add green beans and mushrooms; cook 8 minutes or until mushrooms are lightly browned and beans are softened, stirring occasionally.
3. Meanwhile, whisk orange juice, lime juice, soy sauce and sesame oil in small bowl until well blended.
4. Add shrimp, green bean mixture and bell pepper to large bowl with noodles. Pour dressing over salad; sprinkle with cilantro and sesame seeds, if desired. Toss gently to coat.

Makes 4 servings

Spicy Pasta Salad

- 1 package (12 ounces) uncooked tricolor rotini pasta
- 1¼ cups thick and chunky spicy salsa
- ¾ cup drained canned corn or thawed frozen corn
- ¾ cup canned black beans, rinsed and drained
- 2 green onions, finely chopped
- ⅓ cup chopped fresh cilantro
- ¼ cup mayonnaise
- 1 medium jalapeño pepper, seeded and finely chopped
- ¼ teaspoon salt

1 Cook pasta according to package directions; drain and rinse under cold water.

2 Combine salsa, corn, beans, green onions, cilantro, mayonnaise, jalapeño and salt in large bowl; mix well. Add pasta; stir to coat. Cover and refrigerate at least 1 hour before serving.

Makes 6 servings

TIP This salad is a great way to use small amounts of leftovers in your refrigerator. Add leftover cooked chicken, pork and/or vegetables to the bowl with the pasta for a heartier main dish.

Ravioli Salad

- **1 package (9 ounces) refrigerated cheese ravioli**
- **2 tablespoons extra virgin olive oil**
- **2 teaspoons white wine vinegar**
- **¼ teaspoon salt**
- **⅛ teaspoon black pepper**
- **1 cup halved grape tomatoes *or* 1 chopped tomato**
- **½ cup sliced pimiento-stuffed olives**
- **¼ cup finely chopped celery**
- **1 shallot, finely chopped *or* ¼ cup finely chopped red onion**
- **¼ cup chopped fresh Italian parsley**

1 Cook ravioli according to package directions. Drain well; transfer to large bowl. Set aside to cool 10 minutes.

2 Whisk oil, vinegar, salt and pepper in small bowl until well blended; pour over ravioli. Add tomatoes, olives, celery and shallot; toss gently to coat. Sprinkle with parsley.

Makes 4 to 6 servings

Salmon, Asparagus and Orzo Salad

1 salmon fillet (8 ounces)
1 cup uncooked orzo pasta
3 tablespoons extra virgin olive oil
1 tablespoon white wine vinegar
1½ teaspoons Dijon mustard
½ teaspoon salt
⅛ teaspoon black pepper
8 ounces asparagus, cooked and cut into 2-inch pieces (about 1½ cups)
½ cup dried cranberries
¼ cup sliced green onions

1. Oil grid. Prepare grill for direct cooking over medium heat.
2. Grill salmon about 10 minutes per inch of thickness or until opaque in center. Remove to plate; set aside to cool. Flake salmon into bite-size pieces.
3. Meanwhile, cook orzo according to package directions; drain and cool. Whisk oil, vinegar, mustard, salt and pepper in small bowl until well blended.
4. Combine salmon, orzo, asparagus, cranberries and green onions in large bowl. Pour dressing over salad; toss gently to coat. Refrigerate 30 minutes to 1 hour before serving.

Makes 4 servings

Thai-Style Warm Noodle Salad

- **8 ounces uncooked angel hair pasta**
- **½ cup chunky peanut butter**
- **¼ cup soy sauce**
- **¼ to ½ teaspoon red pepper flakes**
- **2 green onions, thinly sliced**
- **1 carrot, shredded**

1. Cook pasta according to package directions.
2. Meanwhile, whisk peanut butter, soy sauce and red pepper flakes in large bowl until smooth.
3. Drain pasta, reserving 5 tablespoons cooking water. Whisk hot pasta water into peanut butter mixture until smooth.
4. Add pasta to sauce; toss to coat. Stir in green onions and carrot. Serve warm or at room temperature.

Makes 4 servings

NOTES This salad can be prepared a day ahead and served warm or cold. Add leftover cooked chicken, beef, pork or tofu to turn it into a heartier meal.

Mediterranean Chickpea Ramen Salad

- 2 packages (3 ounces each) ramen noodles, broken into small pieces*
- Juice of 1 lemon
- 3 tablespoons olive oil
- 1 teaspoon salt
- ½ teaspoon black pepper
- 1 can (about 15 ounces) chickpeas, rinsed and drained
- 2 tomatoes, diced
- ¾ cup crumbled feta cheese
- ½ cup diced red onion
- ½ English cucumber, seeded and diced
- ¼ cup finely chopped fresh Italian parsley

**Use any flavor; discard seasoning packets.*

1 Cook noodles according to package directions; drain and rinse under cold water.

2 Whisk lemon juice, oil, salt and pepper in large bowl until well blended.

3 Add chickpeas, tomatoes, cheese, onion, cucumber, parsley and noodles; toss to coat.

Makes 6 to 8 servings

White Bean Orzo Salad

- ¾ cup (6 ounces) uncooked orzo pasta
- 1 can (about 15 ounces) navy beans, rinsed and drained
- 1 cup packed fresh spinach, stemmed and coarsely chopped
- ½ cup chopped roasted red peppers
- ¼ cup Italian dressing
- 3 tablespoons capers, rinsed and drained
- 3 tablespoons chopped fresh basil
- ¼ cup crumbled feta cheese

1. Cook pasta according to package directions.
2. Combine beans, spinach, roasted peppers, dressing, capers and basil in large bowl; mix well.
3. Drain pasta; add to salad. Sprinkle with cheese; toss gently to coat.

Makes 4 to 6 servings

Greek Pasta Salad

- 6 cups cooked rotini or penne pasta
- 2 medium tomatoes, diced
- 1½ cups diced cucumber
- 1 medium green bell pepper, diced
- ½ cup crumbled feta cheese
- 12 medium pitted black olives, sliced into thirds
- ¼ cup chopped fresh dill
- Juice of ½ lemon
- ¼ teaspoon salt
- ⅛ teaspoon black pepper

Combine pasta, tomatoes, cucumber, bell pepper, cheese, olives and dill in large bowl. Drizzle with lemon juice; sprinkle with salt and pepper and toss to coat. Cover and refrigerate until ready to serve.

Makes 8 servings

OVEN BAKED

Ramen Reuben Noodle Bake

- **6 cups water**
- **3 packages (3 ounces each) beef-flavored ramen noodles**
- **¼ cup (½ stick) butter, melted**
- **2 cans (14.4 ounces each) shredded sauerkraut, undrained**
- **1 pound thinly sliced deli corned beef, chopped**
- **1½ teaspoons caraway seeds, divided**
- **½ cup Thousand Island dressing**
- **8 slices (6 ounces) Swiss cheese**

1. Preheat oven to 350°F. Spray 3-quart or 13×9-inch baking dish with nonstick cooking spray.
2. Bring water to a boil in large saucepan over high heat. Add noodles and ramen seasoning packets; return to a boil. Cook 2 to 3 minutes or until al dente; drain well.
3. Combine noodles, butter, sauerkraut with liquid, corned beef and 1 teaspoon caraway seeds in large bowl; stir to blend. Spread in prepared baking dish.
4. Cover and bake 20 minutes or until heated through. Drizzle with dressing; top with cheese and remaining ½ teaspoon caraway seeds. Bake, uncovered, 13 to 15 minutes or until cheese is melted and casserole is bubbly.

Makes 8 servings

Baked Chicken and Garlic Orzo

- 1 tablespoon plus 2 teaspoons olive oil, divided
- 4 bone-in chicken breasts, skin removed
- ¼ cup dry white wine
- 1 can (about 14 ounces) chicken broth
- 10 ounces uncooked whole wheat orzo pasta
- 1 cup chopped onion
- ¼ cup water
- 2 tablespoons chopped fresh parsley
- 4 cloves garlic, minced
- 1 teaspoon dried oregano
- ½ teaspoon salt
- 1 teaspoon lemon-pepper seasoning
- ¼ teaspoon paprika
- 1 lemon, cut into 8 wedges

1. Preheat oven to 350°F. Spray 9-inch square baking dish with nonstick cooking spray.
2. Heat 1 tablespoon oil in large skillet over medium-high heat. Add chicken; cook 3 to 5 minutes or until lightly browned. Remove to plate.
3. Add wine to skillet; cook over medium heat 1 minute or until slightly reduced, scraping up browned bits from bottom of skillet.
4. Combine broth, orzo, onion, water, parsley, garlic, oregano, salt and wine mixture in prepared baking dish; mix well. Place chicken breasts over orzo mixture; sprinkle with lemon-pepper seasoning and paprika.
5. Bake, uncovered, 1 hour 10 minutes. Remove chicken to clean plate. Stir remaining 2 teaspoons oil into orzo mixture. Serve chicken over orzo mixture; garnish with lemon wedges.

Makes 4 servings

Little Italy Baked Ziti

- 1 package (16 ounces) uncooked ziti pasta
- 1 pound bulk mild Italian sausage
- 3 cloves garlic, minced
- ¾ cup dry white wine
- 1 jar (24 ounces) marinara sauce
- 1 can (about 14 ounces) diced tomatoes
- 2 tablespoons butter
- 2 cups (8 ounces) shredded mozzarella cheese, divided
- ½ cup coarsely chopped fresh basil, plus additional for garnish
- ¼ cup grated Parmesan cheese

1. Cook pasta in large saucepan of salted boiling water according to package directions until al dente. Drain and return to saucepan; keep warm.
2. Meanwhile, cook sausage in large skillet over medium-high heat about 8 minutes or until no longer pink, stirring to break up meat. Add garlic; cook and stir 1 minute. Add wine; cook 4 minutes or until almost evaporated.
3. Stir in marinara sauce, tomatoes and butter; bring to a boil. Reduce heat to medium-low; cook 20 minutes, stirring occasionally. Preheat broiler. Spray 3-quart or 13×9-inch broilerproof baking dish with nonstick cooking spray.
4. Add sauce mixture, 1 cup mozzarella and ½ cup basil to pasta in saucepan; stir gently to coat. Spread in prepared baking dish; sprinkle with remaining 1 cup mozzarella and Parmesan.
5. Broil 2 to 3 minutes or until cheese begins to bubble and turn golden brown. Garnish with additional basil.

Makes 6 to 8 servings

Cheesy Spinach and Fettuccine Casserole

- 8 ounces uncooked spinach fettuccine
- 1 tablespoon olive oil
- 1½ cups sliced mushrooms
- 2 green onions, finely chopped
- 1 clove garlic, minced
- 1 package (10 ounces) frozen spinach, thawed and squeezed dry*
- 2 tablespoons water
- 1 container (15 ounces) ricotta cheese
- ¾ cup whipping cream
- 1 egg
- ½ teaspoon salt
- ½ teaspoon ground nutmeg
- ½ teaspoon black pepper
- ½ cup (2 ounces) shredded Swiss cheese

**Or, substitute 10 ounces coarsely chopped baby spinach.*

1. Preheat oven to 350°F. Spray 1½-quart baking dish with nonstick cooking spray. Cook pasta according to package directions; drain.
2. Heat oil in medium skillet over medium heat. Add mushrooms, green onions and garlic; cook 5 minutes or until mushrooms are softened, stirring frequently. Add spinach and water; cover and cook about 3 minutes or until spinach is wilted.
3. Whisk ricotta, cream, egg, salt, nutmeg and black pepper in large bowl until well blended. Add pasta and vegetables; stir gently to coat. Spread in prepared baking dish; sprinkle with Swiss cheese.
4. Bake 25 to 30 minutes or until knife inserted halfway into center comes out clean.

Makes 4 to 6 servings

Mushroom Gratin

- **4 tablespoons butter, divided**
- **1 small onion, minced**
- **1 package (8 ounces) sliced cremini mushrooms**
- **2 cloves garlic, minced**
- **4 cups cooked elbow macaroni, rotini or other pasta**
- **2 tablespoons all-purpose flour**
- **1 cup milk**
- **½ teaspoon salt**
- **½ teaspoon black pepper**
- **½ teaspoon dry mustard**
- **½ cup fresh bread crumbs**
- **1 tablespoon olive oil**

1. Preheat oven to 350°F. Spray shallow 2-quart baking dish with nonstick cooking spray.
2. Melt 2 tablespoons butter in large skillet over medium-high heat. Add onion; cook and stir 2 minutes. Add mushrooms and garlic; cook and stir 6 to 8 minutes or until vegetables are soft. Remove from heat; stir in macaroni.
3. Melt remaining 2 tablespoons butter in medium saucepan over low heat. Whisk in flour; cook and stir 2 minutes without browning. Gradually whisk in milk; bring to a boil over medium-high heat, whisking constantly. Reduce heat to maintain a simmer. Add salt, pepper and mustard; whisk 5 to 7 minutes or until sauce thickens.
4. Pour sauce over mushroom mixture in skillet; stir to coat. Spoon into prepared baking dish. Top with bread crumbs; drizzle with oil.
5. Cover and bake 15 minutes. Uncover; bake 10 minutes or until bubbly and browned.

Makes 8 servings

Turkey Veggie Lasagna

- 2 tablespoons olive oil, divided
- 1 pound ground turkey
- 2 cups packed chopped kale
- 1 medium onion, finely chopped
- 3 cloves garlic, minced, divided
- 2 teaspoons salt, divided
- 1 can (28 ounces) crushed tomatoes
- 1 can (about 15 ounces) tomato sauce
- 1 teaspoon Italian seasoning
- 1 package (8 ounces) sliced mushrooms
- 1 medium zucchini (12 ounces), cut in half lengthwise and thinly sliced crosswise
- 1 container (15 ounces) ricotta cheese
- 5 cups (20 ounces) shredded Italian cheese blend or mozzarella cheese, divided
- ½ cup chopped fresh parsley
- 1 egg
- ¼ teaspoon black pepper
- 12 no-boil lasagna noodles

1. Preheat oven to 350°F. Spray 13×9-inch baking dish with nonstick cooking spray. Heat 1 tablespoon oil in large saucepan over medium-high heat. Add turkey, kale, onion, 2 cloves garlic and 1 teaspoon salt; cook and stir 5 minutes or until turkey is no longer pink, stirring to break up meat. Add tomatoes, tomato sauce and Italian seasoning; cook 10 minutes, stirring occasionally.

2. Meanwhile, heat remaining 1 tablespoon oil in large skillet over medium-high heat. Add mushrooms, zucchini and ½ teaspoon salt; cook and stir 5 minutes or until vegetables are tender.

3. Whisk ricotta, 1 cup shredded cheese, parsley, egg, remaining 1 clove garlic, ½ teaspoon salt and pepper in medium bowl until well blended.

4. Spread ¼ cup tomato sauce mixture over bottom of prepared baking dish. Top with 3 noodles. Spread one third of ricotta mixture over noodles; top with 1 cup shredded cheese, 1½ cups sauce and 3 noodles. Spread one third of ricotta mixture over noodles; top with vegetables, 1 cup shredded cheese, 1½ cups sauce and 3 noodles. Spread remaining ricotta mixture over noodles; top with 1 cup shredded cheese and 1 cup sauce. For final layer, top with remaining 3 noodles and remaining sauce. Sprinkle with remaining 1 cup shredded cheese. Cover loosely with greased foil.

5. Bake 30 minutes. Uncover; bake 10 minutes or until sauce is bubbly and hot and cheese is melted. Let stand 10 minutes before serving.

Makes 8 servings

Crab-Artichoke Casserole

- 8 ounces uncooked small shell pasta
- 2 tablespoons butter
- 6 green onions, chopped
- 2 tablespoons all-purpose flour
- 1 cup half-and-half
- 1 teaspoon dry mustard
- ½ teaspoon salt
- ½ teaspoon ground red pepper
- ¼ teaspoon black pepper
- ½ cup (2 ounces) shredded Swiss cheese, divided
- 1 package (about 8 ounces) imitation crabmeat
- 1 can (about 14 ounces) artichoke hearts, drained and cut into bite-size pieces

1. Preheat oven to 350°F. Spray 2-quart baking dish with nonstick cooking spray.
2. Cook pasta according to package directions; drain.
3. Meanwhile, melt butter in large saucepan over medium heat. Add green onions; cook and stir 2 minutes. Add flour; cook and stir 2 minutes. Gradually add half-and-half, whisking constantly until mixture starts to thicken. Whisk in mustard, salt, red pepper and black pepper. Remove from heat; stir in ¼ cup cheese until melted.
4. Combine crabmeat, artichokes and pasta in prepared baking dish. Add sauce mixture; stir gently until blended. Sprinkle with remaining ¼ cup cheese.
5. Bake about 40 minutes or until casserole is hot, bubbly and lightly browned.

Makes 6 servings

Bacon Lovers' Baked Pasta and Cheese

- 8 ounces uncooked fusilli pasta or other corkscrew-shaped pasta
- 12 slices bacon, chopped
- ½ medium onion, chopped
- 2 cloves garlic, minced
- 2 teaspoons dried oregano, divided
- 1 can (8 ounces) tomato sauce
- 1 teaspoon hot pepper sauce (optional)
- 1½ cups (6 ounces) shredded Cheddar or Colby cheese
- ½ cup fresh bread crumbs (from 1 slice of white bread)
- 1 tablespoon butter, melted

1. Preheat oven to 400°F. Cook pasta according to package directions; drain. Meanwhile, cook bacon in large ovenproof skillet over medium heat until crisp. Remove to paper towel-lined plate. Drain all but 2 tablespoons drippings from skillet.
2. Add onion, garlic and 1 teaspoon oregano to skillet; cook and stir 3 minutes or until onion is translucent. Stir in tomato sauce and hot pepper sauce, if desired. Add pasta and cheese; stir to coat.
3. Combine bacon, bread crumbs, remaining 1 teaspoon oregano and butter in small bowl; sprinkle over pasta mixture.
4. Bake 10 to 15 minutes or until hot and bubbly.

Makes 4 servings

Cheeseburger Casserole

- 1 package (16 ounces) uncooked orecchiette pasta
- 1 pound ground beef or ground turkey
- 1 medium onion, chopped
- 1 clove garlic, minced
- 1 teaspoon salt
- ¼ teaspoon black pepper
- 2 tablespoons ketchup
- 1 tablespoon yellow mustard
- 1 can (28 ounces) diced tomatoes
- 2 cups (8 ounces) shredded Cheddar cheese, divided
- 4 slices bacon, cooked and chopped (optional)
- Optional toppings: shredded lettuce, sliced onion, sliced tomatoes, dill pickle slices

1. Preheat oven to 350°F. Spray 13×9-inch baking dish with nonstick cooking spray.
2. Cook pasta in large saucepan of salted boiling water according to package directions for al dente. Drain and transfer large bowl, reserving ¼ cup cooking water.
3. Meanwhile, combine beef, onion, garlic, salt and pepper in large skillet; cook 6 to 8 minutes or until beef is no longer pink, stirring to break up meat. Stir in ketchup and mustard until blended. Stir in tomatoes and reserved pasta water; bring to a simmer.
4. Add beef mixture to pasta; mix well. Stir in ½ cup cheese. Spread in prepared baking dish; top with remaining 1½ cups cheese.
5. Bake about 20 minutes or until cheese is melted and casserole is heated through. Sprinkle with bacon, if desired; let stand 5 minutes before serving. Serve with desired toppings.

Makes 6 to 8 servings

Spaghetti and Vegetable Frittata

- **2 tablespoons olive oil, divided**
- **1 package (8 ounces) sliced mushrooms**
- **1 cup thinly sliced leeks**
- **4 eggs**
- **¼ cup milk**
- **¼ cup grated Parmesan cheese**
- **⅛ teaspoon ground nutmeg**
- **½ teaspoon salt**
- **⅛ teaspoon black pepper**
- **1 package (10 ounces) frozen chopped collard greens, thawed and squeezed dry**
- **2 cups cooked whole grain spaghetti**
- **½ cup (2 ounces) shredded mozzarella cheese**

1. Heat 1 tablespoon oil in large ovenproof skillet over medium-high heat. Add mushrooms and leeks; cook 8 minutes or until vegetables are lightly browned, stirring occasionally.
2. Whisk eggs, milk, Parmesan, nutmeg, salt and pepper in large bowl until well blended. Stir in collard greens, spaghetti and mushroom mixture.
3. Heat remaining 1 tablespoon oil in same skillet over medium-low heat. Add egg mixture; cover and cook 10 minutes or until top is set.
4. Meanwhile, preheat broiler. Sprinkle mozzarella over frittata; broil about 5 inches from heat 3 minutes or until golden brown. Cut into wedges.

Makes 4 servings

Spicy Lasagna Rollers

- 1½ pounds Italian sausage, casings removed
- 1 jar (26 ounces) pasta sauce, divided
- 1 can (8 ounces) tomato sauce
- ½ cup chopped roasted red pepper
- ¾ teaspoon Italian seasoning
- ½ teaspoon red pepper flakes
- 1 container (15 ounces) ricotta cheese
- 1 package (10 ounces) frozen chopped spinach, thawed and squeezed dry
- 2 cups (8 ounces) shredded Italian cheese blend, divided
- 1 cup (4 ounces) shredded Cheddar cheese, divided
- 1 egg, lightly beaten
- 12 lasagna noodles, cooked and drained

1. Preheat oven to 350°F. Spray 13×9-inch baking dish with nonstick cooking spray.
2. Cook sausage in large skillet over medium heat until browned, stirring to break up meat. Drain fat. Stir in ½ cup pasta sauce, tomato sauce, roasted red pepper, seasoning and red pepper flakes.
3. Whisk ricotta, spinach, 1½ cups Italian cheese blend, ½ cup Cheddar and egg in medium bowl until well blended. Spread ¼ cup ricotta mixture over each noodle; top with ⅓ cup sausage mixture. Starting with short ends, tightly roll up noodles. Place rolls, seam sides down, in prepared baking dish. Pour remaining pasta sauce over rolls; sprinkle with remaining ½ cup Italian cheese blend and ½ cup Cheddar. Cover with foil.
4. Bake 30 minutes. Uncover; bake 15 minutes or until sauce is bubbly.

Makes 6 servings

Pumpkin Mac and Cheese

- 1 package (16 ounces) uncooked large elbow macaroni or medium shell pasta
- ½ cup (1 stick) butter, divided
- ¼ cup all-purpose flour
- 1½ cups milk
- 1 teaspoon salt, divided
- ¼ teaspoon ground nutmeg
- ⅛ teaspoon ground red pepper
- 2 cups (8 ounces) shredded Cheddar cheese
- 1 cup (4 ounces) shredded Monterey Jack cheese
- 1 cup canned pumpkin
- 1 cup panko bread crumbs
- ½ cup chopped hazelnuts or walnuts (optional)
- ⅛ teaspoon dried sage
- 1 cup (4 ounces) shredded Chihuahua cheese*

**If Chihuahua cheese is not available, substitute Monterey Jack cheese.*

1. Preheat oven to 350°F. Spray 2-quart baking dish with nonstick cooking spray. Cook macaroni in large saucepan of salted boiling water according to package directions for al dente. Drain and return to saucepan; keep warm.
2. Melt ¼ cup butter in medium saucepan over medium-high heat. Whisk in flour until smooth; cook 1 minute without browning, whisking constantly. Gradually whisk in milk. Add ¾ teaspoon salt, nutmeg and red pepper; cook 2 to 3 minutes or until thickened, whisking frequently. Gradually add Cheddar and Monterey Jack, stirring after each addition until smooth. Add pumpkin; cook 1 minute or until heated through, stirring constantly. Pour sauce over pasta; stir to coat.
3. Melt remaining ¼ cup butter in small skillet over medium-low heat; cook until golden brown. Remove from heat; stir in panko, hazelnuts, if desired, sage and remaining ¼ teaspoon salt.
4. Spread half of pasta in prepared baking dish; sprinkle with ½ cup Chihuahua cheese. Top with remaining pasta; sprinkle with remaining Chihuahua cheese. Top with panko mixture.
5. Bake 25 to 30 minutes or until topping is golden brown and pasta is heated through.

Makes 6 to 8 servings

Artichoke Turkey Noodle Bake

- 8 ounces uncooked wide egg noodles
- 2 tablespoons butter
- ½ cup finely chopped onion
- 1½ tablespoons all-purpose flour
- 1½ cans (12 ounces each) evaporated milk
- ¼ cup cream sherry*
- 1 can (about 14 ounces) stewed tomatoes, drained
- ½ teaspoon salt
- ¼ teaspoon black pepper
- Pinch ground red pepper
- 2½ cups shredded cooked turkey
- 1 can (14 ounces) artichoke hearts, drained and thinly sliced
- 2 cups (8 ounces) shredded Cheddar cheese, divided
- 4 ounces turkey bacon or bacon, cooked and chopped (optional)

***You can substitute ¼ cup dry sherry mixed with 1 teaspoon packed brown sugar for the cream sherry, or use ¼ cup white wine.**

1. Preheat oven to 375°F. Spray 13×9-inch baking dish with nonstick cooking spray.
2. Cook noodles according to package directions; drain and place in large bowl.
3. Meanwhile, melt butter in medium saucepan over medium-high heat. Add onion; cook and stir 3 minutes or until softened. Add flour; cook and stir 1 minute. Gradually add evaporated milk and sherry; cook and stir 5 minutes or until thickened. Stir in tomatoes, salt, black pepper and red pepper; mix well.
4. Pour sauce over noodles. Add turkey, artichokes, 1 cup cheese and bacon, if desired; stir gently to blend. Spread in prepared baking dish; sprinkle with remaining 1 cup cheese.
5. Bake 40 minutes or until cheese is melted and casserole is heated through.

Makes 6 servings

Hearty Manicotti

- 1 container (15 ounces) ricotta cheese
- 2 cups (8 ounces) shredded mozzarella cheese
- ½ cup cottage cheese
- 2 eggs, beaten
- 2 tablespoons grated Parmesan cheese
- ½ teaspoon minced garlic
- ½ teaspoon salt
- ¼ teaspoon black pepper
- 1 package (about 8 ounces) uncooked manicotti shells
- 1 pound ground beef
- 1 jar (about 26 ounces) pasta sauce
- 2 cups water

1. Preheat oven to 375°F.
2. Whisk ricotta, mozzarella, cottage cheese, eggs, Parmesan, garlic, salt and pepper in large bowl until well blended. Fill manicotti shells with cheese mixture; place in 13×9-inch baking dish.
3. Cook beef in large skillet over medium-high heat 6 to 8 minutes or until browned, stirring to break up meat. Drain fat. Stir in pasta sauce and water; bring to a simmer. Pour sauce over filled manicotti shells.
4. Cover and bake 1 hour or until sauce is thickened and manicotti shells are tender.

Makes 6 servings

Pizza Chicken Bake

- **3½ cups uncooked bowtie pasta (farfalle)**
- **1 tablespoon olive oil**
- **1 cup sliced mushrooms**
- **1 jar (26 ounces) herb-flavored pasta sauce**
- **1 teaspoon pizza seasoning blend**
- **12 ounces boneless skinless chicken breasts, cut into 2-inch pieces**
- **1 cup (4 ounces) shredded mozzarella cheese**

1. Preheat oven to 350°F. Spray 2-quart baking dish with nonstick cooking spray. Cook pasta according to package directions until al dente; drain and place in prepared baking dish.
2. Heat oil in large skillet over medium-high heat. Add mushrooms; cook and stir 5 minutes. Remove from heat; stir in pasta sauce and pizza seasoning.
3. Pour half of mushroom mixture over pasta; stir gently to coat. Top with chicken and remaining mushroom mixture.
4. Cover and bake 50 minutes or until chicken is no longer pink in center. Sprinkle with cheese; cover and let stand 5 minutes before serving.

Makes 4 servings

TIP Serve this casserole with grated Parmesan cheese, dried oregano and red pepper flakes so that everyone can add their own pizza seasonings.

Cheesy Italian Noodle Casserole

4 packages (3 ounces each) ramen noodles*
1 pound sweet Italian sausage, casings removed
2 teaspoons olive oil
1 cup diced onion
1 cup diced red bell pepper
1 teaspoon minced garlic
1 can (about 15 ounces) tomato sauce
½ cup thinly sliced fresh basil
2 cups (8 ounces) shredded mozzarella cheese

***Use any flavor; discard seasoning packets.**

1. Preheat oven to 400°F. Spray 13×9-inch baking dish with nonstick cooking spray.
2. Cook noodles according to package directions; drain and rinse under cold water. Transfer to large bowl.
3. Cook sausage in large skillet over medium-high heat 8 minutes or until browned, stirring to break up meat. Drain on paper towel-lined plate. Add to bowl with noodles.
4. Heat oil in same skillet over medium heat. Add onion and bell pepper; cook and stir 6 minutes or until softened. Add garlic; cook and stir 30 seconds. Add vegetable mixture, tomato sauce and basil to bowl with noodles; stir to coat. Spread mixture evenly in prepared baking dish; sprinkle with cheese.
5. Bake 25 to 30 minutes or until cassrole is bubbly and cheese is melted. Let stand 5 minutes before serving.

Makes 8 to 10 servings

Parmesan Alfredo Pasta Bake

- **2 tablespoons plus ½ teaspoon salt, divided**
- **1 package (16 ounces) uncooked fusilli pasta**
- **6 tablespoons (¾ stick) butter**
- **1 clove garlic**
- **1 cup whipping cream**
- **1 cup milk**
- **2 cups shredded Parmesan cheese, divided**
- **1 cup (4 ounces) shredded mozzarella cheese**
- **4 ounces mozzarella cheese, cubed**
- **1 cup panko bread crumbs**
- **2 tablespoons butter, melted**
- **¼ teaspoon Italian seasoning**

1. Preheat oven to 400°F. Spray 3-quart baking dish with nonstick cooking spray.
2. Bring large saucepan of water to a boil; stir in 2 tablespoons salt. Add pasta; cook according to package directions until al dente. Drain pasta, reserving ½ cup cooking water. Return pasta to saucepan.
3. Meanwhile, melt 6 tablespoons butter in medium saucepan over medium heat. Add garlic and remaining ½ teaspoon salt. Stir in cream, milk and reserved ½ cup pasta water; bring to a simmer. Remove from heat; remove and discard garlic clove. Gradually stir in 1 cup Parmesan and shredded mozzarella until smooth and well blended. Pour sauce over pasta; stir gently to coat. Pour into prepared baking dish; fold in cubed mozzarella.
4. Combine panko, remaining 1 cup Parmesan and 2 tablespoons melted butter in medium bowl; mix well. Spread evenly over pasta mixture; sprinkle with Italian seasoning.
5. Bake 15 minutes or until topping is golden brown and pasta is heated through.

Makes 6 to 8 servings

ASIAN INSPIRED

Mushroom Noodle Stir-Fry

- 8 ounces uncooked Chinese egg noodles or spaghetti
- 8 ounces shiitake mushrooms, stemmed and thinly sliced (¼-inch slices)
- Pinch of salt
- 2 tablespoons butter
- 1 tablespoon minced garlic
- 2 teaspoons honey
- ½ cup stir-fry sauce
- 2 to 3 tablespoons water
- 2 green onions, sliced diagonally
- 2 tablespoons grated Parmesan cheese

1 Cook noodles according to package directions; drain and rinse under cold water to stop cooking.

2 Heat large skillet over medium-high heat. Add mushrooms; stir-fry about 5 minutes or until browned. Season with salt. Add butter, garlic and honey; cook and stir 1 minute or until butter is melted and garlic is fragrant but not browned.

3 Add stir-fry sauce, 2 tablespoons water and noodles; cook and stir 2 to 3 minutes or until heated through. Add additional water by teaspoonful, if necessary, to loosen sauce. Divide noodles between serving bowls; top with green onions and cheese.

Makes 2 main-dish or 4 side-dish servings

Soba Teriyaki Bowl

- ¾ cup plus 1 tablespoon cornstarch, divided
- 2 teaspoons salt, divided
- ½ cup plus 2 tablespoons water, divided
- 1 head cauliflower, cut into 1-inch florets
- ¾ cup pineapple juice
- ¾ cup soy sauce
- 2 tablespoons packed brown sugar
- 1 tablespoon lime juice
- 1 teaspoon minced garlic
- 6 ounces uncooked soba noodles
- 5 cups shredded red, green or mixed cabbage *or* 1 package (14 ounces) coleslaw mix
- ½ cup unseasoned rice vinegar
- 1 teaspoon granulated sugar
- 2 green onions, chopped
- 1 tablespoon sesame seeds

1. Preheat oven to 400°F. Spray baking sheet with nonstick cooking spray. Whisk ¾ cup cornstarch and 1 teaspoon salt in medium bowl. Whisk in ½ cup water until smooth. Dip cauliflower into mixture; place in single layer on prepared sheet pan. Bake 20 minutes or until tender.
2. Meanwhile, combine pineapple juice, soy sauce, brown sugar, lime juice and garlic in small saucepan; bring to a simmer over medium-high heat. Whisk remaining 2 tablespoons water into 1 tablespoon cornstarch in small bowl; stir into sauce. Reduce heat to low; cook and stir 5 minutes. Transfer to large bowl; cool slightly. Remove ¼ cup sauce to small bowl; set aside for serving.
3. Cook noodles according to package directions; drain and rinse under cold water until cool. Divide noodles among serving bowls.
4. Combine cabbage, vinegar, granulated sugar and remaining 1 teaspoon salt in medium bowl; mix and squeeze with hands until well blended.
5. Add cauliflower to large bowl of sauce; stir to coat. Divide among serving bowls; drizzle with some of reserved sauce. Serve with cabbage mixture; sprinkle with green onions and sesame seeds.

Makes 4 servings

Spicy Peanut Noodles

- 1 package (about 14 ounces) uncooked Asian stir-fry wheat noodles (udon, hokkien or chow mein)
- 2½ tablespoons creamy peanut butter
- 3 to 4 tablespoons water
- 3 tablespoons soy sauce
- 2 tablespoons unseasoned rice vinegar
- 1 tablespoon packed brown sugar
- 1 tablespoon minced fresh cilantro
- 1 tablespoon chili oil
- ¼ teaspoon red pepper flakes
- ½ cucumber, peeled and julienned
- Fresh cilantro leaves

1 Cook noodles according to package directions; drain.

2 Meanwhile, whisk peanut butter, 3 tablespoons water, soy sauce, vinegar, brown sugar, minced cilantro, chili oil and red pepper flakes in large bowl until smooth and well blended.

3 Add noodles; stir until well coated, adding additional water if necessary to thin sauce. Cover and refrigerate until cold.

4 Divide noodles among serving bowls; top with cucumber and cilantro.

Makes 2 to 4 servings

NOTE You can substitute 1 package (16 ounces) uncooked spaghetti or linguine for the Asian stir-fry noodles. Cook the pasta in a large saucepan of salted boiling water according to package directions for al dente. Drain and place in a large serving bowl, reserving some of the pasta cooking water to use in the sauce.

Ginger Noodles with Sesame Egg Strips

- **2 eggs**
- **1 egg white**
- **6 teaspoons teriyaki sauce, divided**
- **3 teaspoons sesame seeds, toasted,* divided**
- **1 teaspoon dark sesame oil**
- **½ cup chicken broth**
- **1 tablespoon minced fresh ginger**
- **6 ounces Chinese rice noodles or vermicelli noodles, cooked and well drained**
- **⅓ cup sliced green onions**

To toast sesame seeds, cook in small skillet over medium heat about 2 minutes or until seeds begin to pop and turn golden, shaking or stirring frequently.

1. Whisk eggs, egg white, 2 teaspoons teriyaki sauce and 1 teaspoon sesame seeds in medium bowl until well blended.
2. Heat oil in large nonstick skillet over medium heat. Pour in egg mixture; cook 1½ to 2 minutes or until bottom is set. Turn and cook 30 seconds to 1 minute or until cooked through. Slide onto plate; cut into ½-inch strips.
3. Add broth, ginger and remaining 4 teaspoons teriyaki sauce to skillet; bring to a boil over high heat. Reduce heat to medium; stir in noodles. Cook until heated through.
4. Stir in omelet strips and green onions; cook 1 minute or until heated through. Sprinkle with remaining 2 teaspoons sesame seeds just before serving.

Makes 4 servings

Kung Pao Spaghetti

- ½ cup reduced-sodium soy sauce
- ¼ cup dry sherry
- 4 tablespoons water, divided
- 3 tablespoons sugar
- 2 tablespoons chili garlic sauce
- 2 tablespoons red wine vinegar
- 1 tablespoon toasted sesame oil
- 3 tablespoons cornstarch, divided
- 1 package (16 ounces) uncooked spaghetti
- 1 pound boneless skinless chicken breasts, cut into 2-inch pieces
- ¼ teaspoon black pepper
- 2 tablespoons vegetable oil, divided
- 1 tablespoon minced garlic
- ½ cup dry roasted peanuts, coarsely chopped
- 1 bunch green onions (about 6), thickly sliced

1. Whisk soy sauce, sherry, 2 tablespoons water, sugar, chili garlic sauce, vinegar and sesame oil in small bowl until well blended. Stir remaining 2 tablespoons water into 2 tablespoons cornstarch in another small bowl until smooth.
2. Cook pasta in large saucepan of boiling salted water according to package directions for al dente. Drain and place in serving bowl; cover to keep warm.
3. Meanwhile, combine chicken, remaining 1 tablespoon cornstarch and pepper in medium bowl; toss until well coated. Heat 1 tablespoon vegetable oil in large skillet over medium-high heat. Add chicken; cook 5 to 7 minutes or until chicken is browned and cooked through, turning once. Stir in 2 tablespoons soy sauce mixture; cook and stir 1 minute or until chicken is coated. Transfer chicken to plate; wipe out skillet with paper towel.
4. Heat remaining 1 tablespoon vegetable oil in same skillet over medium heat. Add garlic and peanuts; cook and stir 30 seconds or until garlic is fragrant but not browned. Add remaining soy sauce mixture; heat to a simmer. Stir cornstarch mixture; add to skillet. Cook and stir 1 to 2 minutes or until sauce is thickened. Pour over pasta; toss to coat. Stir in peanuts, green onions and chicken.

Makes 4 to 6 servings

Rice Noodles with Broccoli and Tofu

- 1 package (14 ounces) firm or extra firm tofu
- 1 package (8 to 10 ounces) uncooked wide rice noodles
- 2 tablespoons peanut oil
- 3 medium shallots, sliced
- 6 cloves garlic, minced
- 1 jalapeño pepper, minced
- 2 teaspoons minced fresh ginger
- 3 cups broccoli florets
- 3 tablespoons regular soy sauce
- 1 tablespoon sweet soy sauce (kecap manis)*
- 1 to 2 tablespoons fish sauce**
- Fresh basil leaves (optional)

**If sweet soy sauce is not available, substitute 1 tablespoon soy sauce plus 1 tablespoon packed brown sugar.*

***To make this dish vegetarian, look for vegetarian fish sauce or substitute additional soy sauce or fresh lime juice.*

1. Cut tofu crosswise into two pieces. Place tofu on cutting board between layers of paper towels; place weighted saucepan or baking dish on top of tofu. Let stand 30 minutes to drain.
2. Place noodles in large bowl; cover with boiling water. Soak 30 minutes or until soft.
3. Cut tofu into bite-size squares and blot dry. Heat oil in large skillet over medium-high heat. Add tofu to skillet; stir-fry about 5 minutes or until tofu is lightly browned on all sides. Remove to plate.
4. Add shallots, garlic, jalapeño and ginger to skillet; stir-fry 2 minutes. Add broccoli; stir-fry 1 minute. Cover and cook 3 minutes or until broccoli is crisp-tender.
5. Drain noodles; add to skillet and stir to combine. Return tofu to skillet; add soy sauces and fish sauce. Cook and stir 6 to 8 minutes or until noodles are coated and heated through. Garnish with basil.

Makes 4 to 6 servings

Bangkok Peanut Noodles

SAUCE

- 6 tablespoons peanut butter
- ¼ cup soy sauce
- 1 tablespoon unseasoned rice vinegar
- 1 tablespoon packed brown sugar
- 1 tablespoon sriracha sauce
- 2 teaspoons grated fresh ginger
- 2 cloves garlic, minced
- 2 teaspoons dark sesame oil

STIR-FRY

- 1 package (6 ounces) uncooked chow mein stir-fry noodles
- 1 pound boneless skinless chicken breasts, cut into 1-inch pieces *or* 1 package (14 ounces) extra firm tofu, cut into ½-inch cubes
- ½ cup cornstarch
- 3 tablespoons vegetable oil, divided
- 1 red bell pepper, cut into thin strips
- ½ medium onion, thinly sliced
- 2 cups sliced Swiss chard or bok choy
- Chopped roasted peanuts (optional)

1. For sauce, whisk peanut butter, soy sauce, vinegar, brown sugar, sriracha, ginger, garlic and sesame oil in small bowl until smooth.
2. For stir-fry, cook noodles according to package directions; drain and rinse under cold water until cool.
3. Combine chicken and cornstarch in medium bowl; toss to coat. Heat 2 tablespoons vegetable oil in large skillet over medium-high heat. Add chicken; stir-fry 5 minutes or until chicken is golden brown and cooked through. Drain on paper towel-lined plate. Wipe out skillet with paper towel.
4. Heat remaining 1 tablespoon vegetable oil in same skillet over high heat. Add bell pepper and onion; stir-fry 5 minutes or until browned. Add chard; stir-fry 1 minute or until wilted. Add noodles and sauce; cook and stir until noodles are coated with sauce. Add 1 tablespoon water, if needed, to loosen sauce. Return chicken to skillet; stir to coat. Cook just until heated through. Garnish with peanuts.

Makes 4 servings

Soba Stir-Fry

- 8 ounces uncooked soba noodles
- 1 tablespoon vegetable oil
- 2 cups sliced shiitake mushrooms
- 1 medium red bell pepper, cut into thin strips
- 2 whole dried red chiles *or* ¼ teaspoon red pepper flakes
- 1 clove garlic, minced
- 2 cups shredded napa cabbage
- ½ cup vegetable broth
- 2 tablespoons tamari or soy sauce
- 1 tablespoon rice wine or dry sherry
- 2 teaspoons cornstarch
- 1 package (14 ounces) firm tofu, drained and cut into 1-inch cubes
- Salt and black pepper
- 2 green onions, thinly sliced

1. Bring large saucepan of salted water to a boil. Add noodles; return to a boil. Reduce heat to low; cook 3 minutes or until tender. Drain and rinse under cold water until cool.
2. Heat oil in large nonstick skillet over medium-high heat. Add mushrooms, bell pepper, dried chiles and garlic; stir-fry 3 minutes or until mushrooms are tender. Add cabbage; cover and cook 2 minutes or until cabbage is wilted.
3. Whisk broth, tamari and rice wine into cornstarch in small bowl until well blended. Stir sauce into vegetable mixture; cook 2 minutes or until sauce is thickened.
4. Add tofu and noodles; toss gently to coat. Cook 2 minutes or until heated through. Season with salt and black pepper. Sprinkle with green onions. Serve immediately.

Makes 4 servings

Cellophane Noodles with Minced Pork

- 1 package (about 4 ounces) cellophane noodles
- 32 dried shiitake mushrooms
- 2 tablespoons minced fresh ginger
- 2 tablespoons black bean sauce
- 1½ cups chicken broth
- 1 tablespoon dry sherry
- 1 tablespoon soy sauce
- 2 tablespoons vegetable oil
- 6 ounces lean ground pork
- 3 green onions, sliced
- 1 jalapeño or other hot pepper, seeded and finely chopped
- Fresh cilantro sprigs and hot red chile peppers (optional)

1. Place noodles and dried mushrooms in separate bowls; cover each with hot water. Let stand 30 minutes to soften.
2. Drain noodles; cut into 4-inch pieces. Drain mushrooms, squeezing out excess water. Discard stems; cut caps into thin slices.
3. Combine ginger and black bean sauce in small bowl. Whisk broth, sherry and soy sauce in medium bowl until well blended.
4. Heat oil in large skillet over high heat. Add pork; stir-fry 2 minutes or until no longer pink. Add green onions, jalapeño and black bean sauce mixture; cook and stir 1 minute.
5. Add broth mixture, noodles and mushrooms; cook 5 minutes or until most of liquid is absorbed, stirring occasionally. Garnish with cilantro and red peppers.

Makes 4 servings

Japanese Pan Noodles

⅓ cup soy sauce
⅓ cup packed brown sugar
1 tablespoon mirin
1 teaspoon chili garlic sauce
1 tablespoon vegetable or peanut oil
2 cups small broccoli florets (about 2 small crowns or 10 ounces)
2 cups sliced mushrooms
1 cup matchstick carrots (about 2 medium) or shredded carrots
1 tablespoon finely chopped fresh ginger
1 package (14 to 16 ounces) cooked udon noodles*
Black sesame seeds
Fresh cilantro sprigs (optional)

**Or substitute 1 package (16 ounces) dried or fresh udon noodles; cook and drain according to package directions.*

1 Combine soy sauce and brown sugar in small saucepan; bring to a boil over medium-high heat. Reduce heat to medium; cook about 10 minutes or until reduced and thickened slightly, stirring frequently. Remove from heat; stir in mirin and chili garlic sauce until well blended.

2 Heat oil in large saucepan over high heat. Add broccoli and mushrooms; cook and stir 5 minutes or until vegetables are crisp-tender. Add carrots and ginger; cook and stir 1 minute.

3 Add soy sauce mixture and noodles; cook 3 to 5 minutes or until noodles are heated through and most of sauce is absorbed, stirring frequently. Sprinkle with sesame seeds; garnish with cilantro.

Makes 2 to 4 servings

Noodles with Baby Shrimp

- **1 package (3¾ ounces) cellophane noodles**
- **3 green onions**
- **1 tablespoon vegetable oil**
- **1 package (16 ounces) frozen mixed vegetables (such as cauliflower, broccoli and carrots)**
- **1 cup vegetable broth**
- **8 ounces frozen cooked baby shrimp**
- **1 tablespoon soy sauce**
- **2 teaspoons dark sesame oil**
- **¼ teaspoon black pepper**

1. Place noodles in large bowl. Cover with boiling water; let stand 10 to 15 minutes or just until softened. Drain noodles; cut into 5- or 6-inch pieces. Cut green onions into 1-inch pieces.
2. Heat large skillet over high heat about 1 minute or until hot. Drizzle vegetable oil into skillet; heat 30 seconds. Add green onions; stir-fry 1 minute. Add mixed vegetables; stir-fry 2 minutes. Add broth; bring to a boil. Reduce heat to low; cover and cook 5 minutes or until vegetables are crisp-tender.
3. Add shrimp to skillet; cook just until thawed. Stir in noodles, soy sauce, sesame oil and pepper; cook and stir until heated through.

Makes 4 to 6 servings

TIP Cellophane noodles are also called bean thread noodles or glass noodles. These clear, thin noodles are made from mung bean starch and are gluten-free. They are typically sold in packages of 6 to 8 tangled bunches in the Asian section of the supermarket.

Jap Chae (Korean Glass Noodle Stir-Fry)

- **5 ounces cellophane noodles**
- **¼ cup soy sauce**
- **1½ tablespoons dark sesame oil**
- **3 cloves garlic, minced**
- **2 teaspoons sugar**
- **2 tablespoons vegetable oil**
- **1 sweet potato (about 12 ounces), julienned**
- **1 large carrot, julienned or shredded**
- **1 small red onion, halved and thinly sliced**
- **1 small red bell pepper, julienned**
- **1 cup fresh shiitake mushrooms, stemmed and sliced**
- **3 green onions, sliced**
- **1 tablespoon sesame seeds, toasted**

1. Soak noodles in hot water according to package directions. Whisk soy sauce, sesame oil, garlic and sugar in small bowl until well blended.
2. Heat vegetable oil in large skillet over high heat. Add sweet potato; stir-fry 3 minutes. Add carrot, onion, bell pepper and mushrooms; stir-fry 5 minutes or until vegetables are tender.
3. Drain noodles; add to skillet with soy sauce mixture. Cook 2 minutes or until sauce is absorbed. Stir in green onions and sesame seeds. Serve warm, cold or at room temperature.

Makes 6 servings

NOTE This classic Korean dish is typically made with sweet potato noodles (dangmyeon). In this version, chewy cellophane noodles are mixed with ribbons of fresh sweet potato.

TIP This is a great recipe to use your spiralizer if you have one. Use the thin ribbon blade to spiral the sweet potato, carrot, onion and bell pepper, then cut the vegetables into desired lengths.

Soba with Cilantro Peanut Pesto

- 1 cup packed fresh basil leaves
- ½ cup packed fresh cilantro leaves
- ¾ cup dry roasted peanuts, divided
- 1 jalapeño pepper, seeded
- 3 cloves garlic
- 2 teaspoons soy sauce
- 1 tablespoon plus ¾ teaspoon salt, divided
- ½ cup peanut oil
- 1 package (about 12 ounces) uncooked soba noodles
- Chopped fresh cilantro

1 Combine basil, ½ cup cilantro leaves, ½ cup peanuts, jalapeño, garlic, soy sauce and ¾ teaspoon salt in food processor; pulse until coarsely chopped. With motor running, drizzle in oil in thin, steady stream; process until well blended.

2 Bring large saucepan of water to a boil. Add remaining 1 tablespoon salt; stir until dissolved. Add noodles; return to a boil. Reduce heat to low; cook 3 minutes or until tender. Drain and rinse noodles under cold water to cool.

3 Place noodles in medium bowl; add pesto and stir to coat. Chop remaining ¼ cup peanuts; sprinkle over noodles. Garnish with chopped cilantro.

Makes 4 to 6 servings

Vegetarian Rice Noodles

- ½ cup soy sauce
- ⅓ cup sugar
- ¼ cup lime juice
- 2 fresh red Thai chiles *or* 1 large jalapeño pepper, finely chopped
- 8 ounces thin rice noodles (rice vermicelli)
- ¼ cup vegetable oil
- 8 ounces firm tofu, drained and cut into triangles
- 1 jicama (8 ounces), peeled and chopped *or* 1 can (8 ounces) sliced water chestnuts, drained
- 2 medium sweet potatoes (1 pound), peeled and cut into ¼-inch-thick slices
- 2 large leeks, cut crosswise into ¼-inch slices
- ¼ cup chopped dry-roasted peanuts
- 2 tablespoons chopped fresh mint
- 2 tablespoons chopped fresh cilantro

1. Whisk soy sauce, sugar, lime juice and chiles in small bowl until well blended.
2. Place noodles in medium bowl. Cover with hot water; let stand 15 minutes or until softened. Drain noodles; cut into 3-inch lengths.
3. Meanwhile, heat oil in large skillet over medium-high heat. Add tofu; cook 4 minutes per side or until golden brown. Remove to paper towel-lined baking sheet with slotted spatula.
4. Add jicama to skillet; stir-fry 5 minutes or until lightly browned. Remove to baking sheet. Stir-fry sweet potatoes in batches until tender and browned. Remove to baking sheet. Add leeks to skillet; stir-fry 1 minute. Remove to baking sheet.
5. Stir soy sauce mixture; add to skillet and cook until sugar dissolves. Add noodles; toss to coat. Gently stir in tofu, vegetables, peanuts, mint and cilantro; cook until heated through.

Makes 4 servings

Sesame Noodles

- **1 package (16 ounces) uncooked spaghetti**
- **6 tablespoons soy sauce**
- **5 tablespoons toasted sesame oil**
- **3 tablespoons sugar**
- **3 tablespoons rice vinegar**
- **2 tablespoons vegetable oil**
- **3 cloves garlic, minced**
- **1 teaspoon grated fresh ginger**
- **½ teaspoon sriracha**
- **2 green onions, sliced**
- **1 red bell pepper**
- **1 cucumber**
- **1 carrot**
- **Sesame seeds (optional)**

1 Cook pasta in large saucepan of boiling salted water according to package directions for al dente. Drain pasta, reserving 1 tablespoon cooking water.

2 Whisk soy sauce, sesame oil, sugar, vinegar, vegetable oil, garlic, ginger, sriracha and reserved pasta water in large bowl until well blended. Add pasta and green onions; stir to coat. Let stand at least 30 minutes or until pasta has cooled to room temperature and most of sauce is absorbed, stirring occasionally.

3 Meanwhile, cut bell pepper into thin strips. Peel cucumber and carrot; shred into long strands with julienne peeler or cut into thin strips. Stir vegetables into pasta. Serve at room temperature or refrigerate until ready to serve. Top with sesame seeds, if desired.

Makes 6 to 8 servings

Spicy Chicken Rigatoni

- 2 tablespoons olive oil
- 2 cloves garlic, minced
- ½ teaspoon red pepper flakes
- ½ teaspoon black pepper
- 8 ounces boneless skinless chicken breasts, cut into thin strips
- 1 cup marinara sauce
- ¾ cup Alfredo sauce
- 1 package (16 ounces) mezzo rigatoni or penne pasta, cooked until al dente
- ¾ cup frozen peas, thawed
- Grated Parmesan cheese (optional)

1. Heat oil in large saucepan over medium-high heat. Add garlic, red pepper flakes and black pepper; cook and stir 1 minute. Add chicken; cook and stir 4 minutes or until cooked through.
2. Add marinara sauce and Alfredo sauce; stir until blended. Reduce heat to medium-low; cook 10 minutes, stirring occasionally.
3. Add pasta and peas; stir gently to coat. Cook 2 minutes or until heated through. Sprinkle with cheese, if desired.

Makes 4 servings

Spaghetti Aglio e Olio

8 ounces uncooked spaghetti or thin spaghetti
⅓ cup plus 1 tablespoon olive oil, divided
1 cup fresh Italian or French bread crumbs*
4 cloves garlic, very thinly sliced
¾ teaspoon salt
½ teaspoon red pepper flakes
½ cup chopped fresh Italian parsley
¾ cup shredded Parmesan cheese, divided

To make fresh bread crumbs, tear 2 ounces bread into pieces; process in food processor until coarse crumbs form.

1 Cook pasta according to package directions.

2 Meanwhile, heat 1 tablespoon oil in large skillet over medium heat. Add bread crumbs; cook 4 to 5 minutes or until golden brown, stirring frequently. Transfer to small bowl; set aside.

3 Add remaining ⅓ cup oil, garlic, salt and red pepper flakes to same skillet; cook about 3 minutes or until edges of garlic just begin to brown.

4 Drain pasta, reserving ½ cup pasta cooking water. Add pasta and parsley to skillet; stir to coat with oil mixture. Add some of reserved pasta water to moisten pasta, if necessary. Stir in bread crumbs and ½ cup cheese. Sprinkle with remaining ¼ cup cheese.

Makes 4 servings

Penne with Ricotta, Tomatoes and Basil

- 1 package (16 ounces) uncooked penne pasta
- 2 cans (about 14 ounces each) Italian-style diced tomatoes, drained
- 1 container (15 ounces) ricotta cheese
- ⅔ cup chopped fresh basil
- ¼ cup extra virgin olive oil
- 1 tablespoon balsamic vinegar
- 1 clove garlic, minced
- 1 teaspoon salt
- ¼ teaspoon red pepper flakes or black pepper
- Grated Parmesan cheese

1. Cook pasta according to package directions; drain.
2. Meanwhile, combine tomatoes, ricotta, basil, oil, vinegar, garlic, salt and red pepper flakes in large bowl; mix well.
3. Add pasta to ricotta mixture; toss gently to coat. Sprinkle with Parmesan. Serve immediately.

Makes 4 servings

Easy Taco Pasta Skillet

1 pound ground beef
1 onion, chopped
1 package (about 1 ounce) taco seasoning mix
2 cups water
1 jar (16 ounces) medium salsa
1 can (4 ounces) diced green chiles
¼ teaspoon salt
8 ounces uncooked rotini pasta
Shredded Cheddar or Mexican blend cheese (optional)

1 Cook beef and onion in large skillet over medium-high heat 6 to 8 minutes or until browned, stirring frequently. Drain fat. Add taco seasoning mix; cook and stir 1 minute.

2 Stir in water, salsa, chiles and salt; mix well. Stir in pasta; bring to a simmer. Reduce heat to low; cover and cook about 12 minutes or until pasta is tender.

3 Serve immediately with cheese, if desired.

Makes 6 servings

Orecchiette with Sausage and Broccoli Rabe

- 1 tablespoon olive oil
- 12 ounces bulk mild Italian sausage
- 3 cloves garlic, minced
- ¼ teaspoon red pepper flakes
- 4 cups chicken broth, divided
- ¾ teaspoon salt
- 1 package (16 ounces) uncooked orecchiette pasta
- 1 bunch broccoli rabe (about 1 pound), tough stems removed, cut into 2-inch-long pieces
- ¾ cup grated Parmesan cheese, divided
- Juice of 1 lemon

1 Heat oil in large saucepan or Dutch oven over medium-high heat. Add sausage; cook 8 minutes or until browned, stirring to break up meat. Add garlic and red pepper flakes; cook and stir 1 minute. Add 2 tablespoons broth, cook 1 minute, scraping up browned bits from bottom of saucepan.

2 Stir in remaining broth and salt; bring to a boil. Add pasta, stirring to separate pieces as much as possible. (Orecchiette pasta often sticks together in stacks in the package and during cooking.) Reduce heat to medium; cover and cook 10 minutes, stirring occasionally to prevent pasta from sticking.

3 Add broccoli rabe; stir to wilt and blend with pasta. Cover and cook 4 minutes or until pasta is tender and liquid is absorbed, stirring occasionally.

4 Stir in ½ cup cheese and lemon juice; mix well. Serve immediately with remaining ¼ cup cheese.

Makes 4 to 6 servings

Asian Chicken and Noodles

- **8 ounces uncooked thin pad Thai rice noodles**
- **1 tablespoon vegetable oil**
- **1 pound boneless skinless chicken breasts, cut into 1×½-inch pieces**
- **2 cloves garlic, minced**
- **1 bottle or jar (about 12 ounces) stir-fry sauce**
- **¼ cup water**
- **2 tablespoons packed brown sugar**
- **1 package (16 ounces) frozen stir-fry vegetable blend (do not thaw)**

1. Cook or soak noodles according to package directions until almost tender.
2. Heat oil in large skillet over high heat. Add chicken; cook and stir 4 minutes or until no longer pink. Add garlic; cook and stir 30 seconds. Remove chicken to plate.
3. Add stir-fry sauce, water and brown sugar to skillet; cook 2 minutes, scraping up browned bits from bottom of skillet. Stir in noodles, vegetables and chicken; cook until vegetables are tender and noodles are saucy.

Makes 4 servings

Turkey Vegetable Chili Mac

- **1 tablespoon vegetable oil**
- **12 ounces ground turkey**
- **½ cup chopped onion**
- **2 cloves garlic, minced**
- **1 can (about 15 ounces) black beans, rinsed and drained**
- **1 can (about 14 ounces) Mexican-style stewed tomatoes, undrained**
- **1 can (about 14 ounces) diced tomatoes**
- **1 cup frozen corn**
- **1 teaspoon Mexican seasoning**
- **½ teaspoon salt**
- **½ cup uncooked elbow macaroni**
- **Sour cream (optional)**
- **Finely chopped fresh cilantro or green onions (optional)**

1. Heat oil in large nonstick saucepan over medium heat. Add turkey, onion and garlic; cook 5 minutes or until turkey is no longer pink, stirring to break up meat.
2. Stir in beans, tomatoes with juice, corn, Mexican seasoning and salt; bring to a boil over high heat. Reduce heat to low; cover and simmer 15 minutes, stirring occasionally.
3. Meanwhile, cook pasta according to package directions. Drain pasta; stir into turkey mixture. Cook, uncovered, 2 to 3 minutes or until heated through. Top with sour cream and cilantro, if desired.

Makes 4 servings

Linguine with Clam Sauce

- **8 ounces uncooked linguine**
- **2 tablespoons olive oil**
- **1 cup chopped onion**
- **1 can (about 14 ounces) Italian-style stewed tomatoes, drained and chopped**
- **2 cloves garlic, minced**
- **2 teaspoons dried basil**
- **½ cup dry white wine or chicken broth**
- **1 can (10 ounces) whole baby clams, drained, juice reserved**
- **⅓ cup chopped fresh parsley**
- **¼ teaspoon salt**
- **¼ teaspoon black pepper**

1. Cook pasta according to package directions; drain.
2. Meanwhile, heat oil in large skillet over medium heat. Add onion; cook and stir 3 minutes or until softened. Add tomatoes, garlic and basil; cook and stir 3 minutes. Stir in wine and reserved clam juice; bring to a boil. Reduce heat to low; cook 5 minutes.
3. Stir in clams, parsley, salt and pepper; cook 1 to 2 minutes or until heated through. Spoon sauce over hot pasta; toss gently to coat. Serve immediately.

Makes 4 servings

Speedy Ravioli Soup

- **8 ounces mild Italian sausage, casings removed**
- **½ cup chopped onion**
- **1 clove garlic, crushed**
- **2 cans (about 14 ounces each) chicken broth**
- **2 cups water**
- **1 package (9 ounces) frozen mini cheese-filled ravioli**
- **1 can (about 15 ounces) chickpeas, rinsed and drained**
- **1 can (about 14 ounces) diced tomatoes with green chiles**
- **¾ teaspoon dried oregano**
- **½ teaspoon salt**
- **½ teaspoon black pepper**
- **1 cup baby spinach**
- **Grated Parmesan cheese**

1 Cook sausage, onion and garlic in large saucepan or Dutch oven over medium heat 5 minutes or until sausage is cooked through, stirring to break up meat. Drain fat. Remove to medium bowl.

2 Add broth and water to saucepan; bring to a boil over medium-high heat. Add ravioli; cook 4 to 5 minutes or until tender.

3 Return sausage mixture to saucepan with chickpeas, tomatoes, oregano, salt and pepper; cook 5 minutes until heated through. Stir in spinach; cook 1 minute or until wilted. Sprinkle with cheese.

Makes 8 servings

Quick Pasta Puttanesca

- **1 package (16 ounces) uncooked spaghetti or linguine**
- **3 tablespoons plus 1 teaspoon olive oil, divided**
- **¼ to 1 teaspoon red pepper flakes***
- **1 tablespoon dried minced onion**
- **1 teaspoon minced garlic**
- **2 cans (about 6 ounces each) chunk light tuna packed in water, drained**
- **1 can (28 ounces) diced tomatoes**
- **1 can (8 ounces) tomato sauce**
- **24 pitted Kalamata or black olives**
- **2 tablespoons capers, drained**

For a mildly spicy dish, use ¼ teaspoon red pepper flakes. For a very spicy dish, use 1 teaspoon red pepper flakes.

1 Cook spaghetti according to package directions; drain and return to saucepan. Add 1 teaspoon oil; toss to coat. Cover to keep warm.

2 Heat remaining 3 tablespoons oil in large skillet over medium-high heat. Add red pepper flakes; cook and stir until sizzling. Add onion and garlic; cook and stir 1 minute. Add tuna; cook and stir 2 to 3 minutes. Add tomatoes, tomato sauce, olives and capers; cook until sauce is heated through, stirring frequently.

3 Add sauce to pasta; stir to coat. Serve immediately.

Makes 6 to 8 servings

Bowtie Pasta with Chicken and Bacon

- **3 cups uncooked bowtie pasta (farfalle)**
- **4 slices bacon, chopped**
- **1 pound boneless skinless chicken breasts, cut into 1-inch pieces**
- **1 can (about 14 ounces) Italian-style diced tomatoes**
- **¼ teaspoon black pepper**
- **½ cup chicken broth or water**
- **4 ounces cream cheese, cubed**
- **4 tablespoons grated Parmesan cheese, divided**

1 Cook pasta in large saucepan of boiling salted water according to package directions for al dente. Drain pasta and return to saucepan; cover to keep warm.

2 Meanwhile, cook bacon in large skillet over medium-high heat until almost crisp. Remove to paper towel-lined plate. Drain all but 1 tablespoon drippings from skillet.

3 Add chicken to skillet; cook over medium heat about 6 minutes or until cooked through, stirring occasionally. Add tomatoes and pepper; cook and stir 1 minute. Add broth, cream cheese and 2 tablespoons Parmesan; cook and stir about 3 minutes or until cream cheese is melted.

4 Add chicken mixture to pasta; toss gently to coat. Sprinkle with remaining 2 tablespoons Parmesan.

Makes 4 servings

Baked Gnocchi

1 package (about 17 ounces) gnocchi
⅓ cup olive oil
3 cloves garlic, minced
1 package (10 ounces) fresh spinach
1 can (about 14 ounces) diced tomatoes
1 teaspoon Italian seasoning
½ teaspoon salt
¼ teaspoon black pepper
½ cup grated Parmesan cheese
½ cup (2 ounces) shredded mozzarella cheese

1. Preheat oven to 350°F. Spray 2½-quart baking dish with nonstick cooking spray.
2. Cook gnocchi according to package directions; drain.
3. Meanwhile, heat oil in large skillet over medium heat. Add garlic; cook and stir 30 seconds. Stir in spinach; cover and cook 2 minutes or until wilted. Add tomatoes, Italian seasoning, salt and pepper; cook 5 minutes, stirring occasionally. Gently stir in gnocchi. Transfer to prepared baking dish; sprinkle with Parmesan and mozzarella.
4. Bake 20 to 30 minutes or until casserole is bubbly and cheese is melted.

Makes 4 to 6 servings

Turkey Shanghai

- **1 tablespoon vegetable oil**
- **12 ounces turkey tenderloin, thinly sliced***
- **1 cup thinly sliced carrots**
- **½ cup sliced green onions**
- **3 cloves garlic, minced**
- **4 cups chicken broth**
- **6 ounces uncooked angel hair pasta**
- **2 cups frozen French-style green beans**
- **6 tablespoons stir-fry sauce**
- **1 teaspoon dark sesame oil**

If turkey tenderloin is not available, substitute boneless skinless chicken breasts or pork tenderloin.

1. Heat oil in large skillet over medium heat. Add turkey and carrots; cook and stir 5 minutes or until turkey is no longer pink. Add green onions and garlic; cook and stir 2 minutes.
2. Add chicken broth to skillet; bring to a boil over high heat. Stir in pasta; return to a boil. Reduce heat to low; cook 5 minutes, stirring frequently.
3. Add green beans to skillet; cook 2 to 3 minutes or just until pasta is tender, stirring occasionally.
4. Remove from heat; stir in stir-fry sauce and sesame oil. Let stand 5 minutes before serving.

Makes 4 servings

One-Pot Mediterranean Pasta

6 ounces uncooked rotini pasta
1 can (about 15 ounces) navy or cannellini beans
8 ounces grape tomatoes, halved
3 cups packed fresh spinach (3 ounces), stemmed and coarsely chopped
5 slices hard salami (2 ounces), cut into thin strips
20 pitted Kalamata olives, coarsely chopped
⅓ to ½ cup olive oil vinaigrette
3 to 4 tablespoons chopped fresh basil
4 ounces crumbled feta cheese with basil and sun-dried tomatoes

1. Cook pasta in large saucepan of boiling salted water according to package directions for al dente.
2. Meanwhile, drain beans in colander. Drain cooked pasta into beans; shake off excess liquid.
3. Return pasta with beans to saucepan. Add tomatoes, spinach, salami, olives, ⅓ cup vinaigrette and basil; toss gently to coat and wilt spinach slightly. Top with cheese; toss again. Add additional vinaigrette if pasta seems dry. Cover and let stand 5 minutes before serving.

Makes 6 servings

NOTE Refrigerate leftovers to eat as a salad the next day; add additional dressing as needed.

Chicken with Parmesan Fettuccine

2 tablespoons butter, divided
1 pound boneless skinless chicken breasts, cut into bite-size pieces
1 clove garlic, minced
3½ cups chicken broth
6 ounces uncooked fettuccine, broken in half
½ cup whipping cream
½ cup grated Parmesan cheese
½ cup finely chopped green onions
¼ teaspoon black pepper

1 Melt 1 tablespoon butter in large saucepan over medium heat. Add chicken and garlic; cook and stir 3 minutes or until chicken is cooked through. Remove to plate; cover to keep warm.

2 Add broth to saucepan; bring to a boil over high heat. Stir in pasta; return to a boil. Reduce heat to medium-low; cover and cook 10 minutes or just until tender, stirring occasionally. Drain pasta and return to saucepan, reserving ¼ cup broth.

3 Add chicken and cream to pasta; mix well. Gradually stir in cheese. Stir in green onions, pepper and remaining 1 tablespoon butter; cook 2 minutes or until thickened. Add reserved broth to thin sauce, if necessary.

Makes 4 servings

Linguine with Herbs, Tomatoes and Capers

- 1 package (9 ounces) refrigerated linguine
- 2 tablespoons olive oil
- 2 cups chopped fresh tomatoes
- 2 cloves garlic, minced
- ¼ cup finely chopped green onions
- 3 tablespoons capers, drained
- 2 tablespoons finely chopped fresh basil
- ¼ teaspoon salt
- ⅛ teaspoon black pepper
- ½ cup shredded Parmesan cheese (optional)

1 Cook pasta according to package directions; drain.

2 Meanwhile, heat oil in large skillet over medium-high heat. Add tomatoes and garlic; cook 3 minutes or until tomatoes begin to soften, stirring frequently. Stir in green onions, capers and basil. Season with salt and pepper.

3 Add pasta to skillet; toss with tomato mixture. Sprinkle with cheese, if desired.

Makes 4 servings

Pesto and Tortellini Soup

- 1 package (9 ounces) refrigerated cheese tortellini
- 3 cans (about 14 ounces each) chicken or vegetable broth
- 1 jar (7 ounces) roasted red peppers, drained and thinly sliced
- ¾ cup frozen green peas
- 3 to 4 cups packed stemmed fresh spinach
- 2 tablespoons prepared pesto
- Grated Parmesan cheese (optional)

1 Cook tortellini according to package directions; drain.

2 Meanwhile, bring broth to a boil in large saucepan over high heat. Add cooked tortellini, roasted peppers and peas; return to a boil. Reduce heat to medium; cook 1 minute.

3 Remove from heat; stir in spinach and pesto. Serve with cheese, if desired.

Makes 6 servings

SAUCY PASTA

Pasta Primavera with Ricotta

- 6 ounces uncooked fettuccine
- 1 cup ricotta cheese
- ½ cup milk
- 1 zucchini
- 1 yellow squash
- 1 red bell pepper
- 4 teaspoons olive oil
- 1 clove garlic, minced
- ½ teaspoon red pepper flakes
- 1 cup fresh or frozen peas
- ½ teaspoon salt
- 1 teaspoon Italian seasoning
- ½ cup grated Parmesan cheese

1. Cook pasta according to package directions for al dente. Drain and return to saucepan; keep warm. Whisk ricotta and milk in small bowl until well blended.
2. Spiral zucchini and yellow squash with fine spiral blade; spiral bell pepper with spiral slicing blade.* Cut vegetables into desired lengths.
3. Heat oil in large skillet over medium heat. Add garlic and red pepper flakes; cook and stir 1 minute. Add zucchini, yellow squash, bell pepper, peas, salt and Italian seasoning; cook and stir 5 minutes or until vegetables are crisp-tender.
4. Combine pasta, vegetables and ricotta mixture in large bowl; toss gently to coat. Sprinkle with Parmesan just before serving.

**If you don't have a spiralizer, cut vegetables into long, thin strips with sharp knife.*

Makes 4 servings

Ravioli with Tomato Sauce and Spinach

3 tablespoons olive oil
3 cloves garlic, minced
1 teaspoon Italian seasoning
Pinch red pepper flakes
2 tablespoons tomato paste
1 can (28 ounces) whole peeled tomatoes, coarsely chopped or crushed with hands
½ teaspoon sugar
½ teaspoon salt
¼ teaspoon black pepper
1 teaspoon balsamic vinegar
2 cups chopped stemmed fresh spinach
2 packages (9 ounces) refrigerated fresh cheese ravioli
½ cup chopped fresh basil
Grated Parmesan cheese (optional)

1 Heat oil in large saucepan over medium heat. Add garlic; cook 4 minutes, stirring occasionally. Add Italian seasoning and red pepper flakes; cook and stir 1 minute. Add tomato paste; cook and stir 2 minutes or until it begins to caramelize. Stir in tomatoes, sugar, salt and black pepper; bring to a boil. Reduce heat to medium-low; cook 20 minutes, stirring occasionally.

2 Stir in vinegar until blended. Stir in spinach; bring to a simmer over medium-high heat. Reduce heat to medium-low; cook about 5 minutes or until spinach is tender.

3 Meanwhile, cook ravioli according to package directions.

4 Stir basil into sauce. Drain ravioli; add to sauce. Cook 1 minute, stirring gently to coat. Serve with cheese, if desired.

Makes 6 servings

Asian Pesto Noodles

Spicy Asian Pesto (recipe follows)
1 pound large raw shrimp, peeled and deveined
12 ounces uncooked soba noodles

1. Prepare Spicy Asian Pesto.
2. Combine shrimp and ¾ cup pesto in medium bowl or resealable food storage bag; stir to coat. Marinate at room temperature 15 minutes or cover and refrigerate up to 1 hour.
3. Cook noodles according to package directions; drain. Preheat broiler.
4. Thread shrimp onto metal skewers. (If using wooden skewers, soak in water at least 30 minutes to prevent burning.) Broil about 3 minutes per side or until shrimp are opaque.
5. Combine noodles and remaining pesto in large bowl; toss to coat. Top with shrimp.

Makes 4 servings

Spicy Asian Pesto

3 cups fresh basil leaves
3 cups fresh cilantro leaves
3 cups fresh mint leaves
¾ cup peanut oil
3 tablespoons sugar
2 to 3 tablespoons lime juice
5 cloves garlic, chopped
2 teaspoons fish sauce *or* 1 teaspoon salt
1 serrano pepper, chopped

Combine all ingredients in blender or food processor; blend until smooth.

Makes 2½ cups

Vegetable Spaghetti Sauce with Meatballs

- 2 tablespoons olive oil
- 1½ cups sliced mushrooms
- ½ cup plus 2 tablespoons finely chopped onion, divided
- ½ cup chopped carrot
- ½ cup chopped green bell pepper
- 2 cloves garlic, minced
- 2 cans (about 14 ounces each) stewed tomatoes, undrained
- 1 can (6 ounces) tomato paste
- 2½ teaspoons Italian seasoning, divided
- 1¼ teaspoons salt, divided
- ¼ teaspoon black pepper
- 1 egg white
- 2 tablespoons fine dry bread crumbs
- 8 ounces ground beef
- 4 cups hot cooked spaghetti

1. Heat oil in large saucepan over medium heat. Add mushrooms, ½ cup onion, carrot, bell pepper and garlic; cook and stir 4 to 5 minutes or until vegetables are crisp-tender. Stir in tomatoes with juice, tomato paste, 2 teaspoons Italian seasoning, ¾ teaspoon salt and black pepper; bring to a boil over medium-high heat. Reduce heat to medium-low; cover and simmer 20 minutes, stirring occasionally.
2. Preheat oven to 375°F. Combine egg white, bread crumbs, remaining 2 tablespoons onion, ½ teaspoon salt and ½ teaspoon Italian seasoning in medium bowl. Add beef; mix until well blended. Shape into 16 meatballs; place in 11×7-inch baking pan.
3. Bake meatballs 18 to 20 minutes or until beef is cooked through. Drain on paper towel-lined plate.
4. Add meatballs to sauce; return to a boil over medium-high heat. Reduce heat to medium-low; simmer, uncovered, 10 minutes or until sauce thickens slightly, stirring occasionally. Serve over spaghetti.

Makes 4 servings

Cheese Ravioli with Wild Mushroom Sauce

- 2 tablespoons olive oil
- 1 medium onion, chopped
- 1 clove garlic, minced
- 8 ounces firm tofu
- 1½ cups ricotta cheese
- 1 cup grated Parmesan cheese, divided
- ½ teaspoon dried rosemary
- ¼ teaspoon salt
- 64 wonton wrappers (about 1⅓ packages)
- Wild Mushroom Sauce (page 167)

1 Heat oil in small skillet over medium heat. Add onion and garlic; cook and stir 5 minutes or until tender. Place in medium bowl.

2 Drain tofu on paper towels. Cut into 1-inch cubes. Combine tofu, ricotta, ⅓ cup Parmesan, rosemary and salt in food processor; process until smooth. Stir into onion mixture.

3 Working with eight wonton wrappers at a time (keep remaining wrappers covered with plastic wrap), place about 1 tablespoon cheese mixture in center of each wrapper. Brush edges of wrappers with water. Place second wrapper over filling; press edges together to seal. Place on baking sheet; cover with plastic wrap. Repeat with remaining wrappers and cheese mixture.

4 Prepare Wild Mushroom Sauce; keep warm over low heat.

5 Bring 3 quarts water to a boil in large saucepan or Dutch oven over high heat. Add eight ravioli to boiling water. Reduce heat to medium-high; boil gently 3 to 4 minutes or until ravioli float to surface and are just tender. Remove to warm platter with slotted spoon; repeat with remaining ravioli. Serve ravioli with mushroom sauce and remaining ⅔ cup cheese.

Makes 6 to 8 servings

Wild Mushroom Sauce

- **3 tablespoons olive oil**
- **12 ounces fresh shiitake mushrooms, sliced**
- **6 ounces cremini or button mushrooms, sliced**
- **1½ cups sliced green onions**
- **1 tablespoon dried basil**
- **½ teaspoon dried thyme**
- **3 cups vegetable broth, divided**
- **1½ tablespoons cornstarch**
- **2 tablespoons minced parsley**
- **½ teaspoon salt**
- **4 to 6 dashes hot pepper sauce**

1 Heat oil in large skillet over medium heat. Add mushrooms, green onions, basil and thyme; cook and stir 5 minutes or until mushrooms release liquid. Cook 10 minutes or until mushrooms have darkened and all liquid is evaporated, stirring occasionally. Add 2¾ cups broth; bring to a boil. Reduce heat to medium-low; simmer, uncovered, 10 to 12 minutes or until broth is reduced by one-third. Return liquid to a boil.

2 Stir cornstarch into remaining ¼ cup broth in small bowl until smooth. Add to mushroom mixture; boil 1 to 2 minutes or until sauce is thickened, stirring constantly. Stir in parsley, salt and hot pepper sauce.

Makes about 3 cups

Classic Pesto with Linguine

- **12 ounces uncooked linguine**
- **2 tablespoons butter**
- **¼ cup extra virgin olive oil**
- **2 tablespoons pine nuts**
- **1 cup tightly packed fresh basil leaves**
- **2 cloves garlic**
- **¼ teaspoon salt**
- **¼ cup grated Parmesan cheese**
- **1½ tablespoons grated Romano cheese**

1 Cook pasta according to package directions; drain and place in large serving bowl. Add butter; toss to coat. Cover to keep warm.

2 Meanwhile, cook pine nuts in small skillet over medium-low heat 30 to 45 seconds or until lightly browned, shaking skillet constantly. Remove to plate; let cool to room temperature.

3 Combine toasted pine nuts, basil, garlic and salt in food processor or blender; pulse until ingredients are coarsely chopped. With motor running, drizzle in oil in slow, steady stream; process until pesto is well blended and pine nuts are finely chopped.

4 Transfer pesto to small bowl; stir in Parmesan and Romano.*

5 Add pesto to pasta; toss to coat. Serve immediately.

**Sauce can be stored at this point; place in airtight container and pour thin layer of olive oil over pesto. Cover and refrigerate up to 1 week. Bring to room temperature before using.*

Makes 4 servings

Potato Gnocchi with Tomato Sauce

- **2 pounds baking potatoes (3 or 4 large)**
- **Tomato Sauce (page 171) or prepared meatless pasta sauce**
- **⅔ to 1 cup all-purpose flour, divided**
- **1 egg yolk**
- **½ teaspoon salt**
- **⅛ teaspoon ground nutmeg (optional)**
- **Grated Parmesan cheese**
- **Slivered fresh basil**

1. Preheat oven to 425°F. Pierce potatoes several times with fork. Bake 1 hour or until soft. Meanwhile, prepare Tomato Sauce.
2. Cut potatoes in half lengthwise; cool slightly. Scoop out potato flesh into medium bowl; discard skins. Mash potatoes until smooth. Add ⅓ cup flour, egg yolk, salt and nutmeg, if desired; mix well to form dough.
3. Turn out dough onto well-floured surface. Knead in enough remaining flour to form smooth dough. Divide dough into four pieces; roll each piece into ¾- to 1-inch-wide rope with hands on lightly floured surface. Cut each rope into 1-inch pieces; gently press thumb into center of each piece to make indentation. Transfer gnocchi to lightly floured kitchen towel; spread in single layer to prevent sticking.
4. Bring 4 quarts of salted water to a gentle boil in large saucepan over high heat. To test cooking time, drop several gnocchi into water; cook 1 minute or until gnocchi float to surface. Remove from water with slotted spoon and taste for doneness. (If gnocchi start to dissolve, shorten cooking time by several seconds.) Cook remaining gnocchi in batches, removing with slotted spoon to warm serving dish.
5. Serve gnocchi with sauce; sprinkle with cheese and basil.

Makes 4 servings

Tomato Sauce

- 2 tablespoons olive oil or butter
- 1 clove garlic, minced
- 2 pounds ripe plum tomatoes, peeled, seeded and chopped
- 1 teaspoon sugar
- ¼ cup finely chopped prosciutto or cooked ham (optional)
- 1 tablespoon finely chopped fresh basil
- Salt and black pepper

Heat oil in medium saucepan over medium heat. Add garlic; cook and stir 30 seconds or until fragrant. Add tomatoes and sugar; cook 10 minutes or until most liquid has evaporated, stirring occasionally. Stir in prosciutto, if desired, and basil; cook 2 minutes. Season with salt and pepper to taste.

Makes about 2 cups

Angel Hair Pasta with Seafood Sauce

- **8 ounces uncooked angel hair pasta**
- **2 teaspoons olive oil**
- **½ cup chopped onion**
- **2 cloves garlic, minced**
- **3 pounds plum tomatoes, seeded and chopped**
- **¼ cup chopped fresh basil**
- **2 tablespoons chopped fresh oregano**
- **1 teaspoon red pepper flakes**
- **½ teaspoon sugar**
- **½ teaspoon salt**
- **2 bay leaves**
- **8 ounces firm whitefish, such as sea bass, monkfish or grouper, cut into ¾-inch pieces**
- **8 ounces bay scallops or shucked oysters**
- **2 tablespoons chopped fresh Italian parsley**

1. Cook pasta according to package directions; drain.
2. Meanwhile, heat oil in large skillet over medium heat. Add onion and garlic; cook and stir 3 minutes or until onion is translucent. Add tomatoes, basil, oregano, red pepper flakes, sugar, salt and bay leaves; cook over low heat 15 minutes, stirring occasionally.
3. Add fish and scallops; cook 3 to 4 minutes or until fish begins to flake when tested with fork and scallops are opaque. Remove and discard bay leaves.
4. Combine pasta and seafood sauce in large bowl; toss gently to coat. Sprinkle with parsley.

Makes 6 servings

Ravioli with Spinach Pesto and Chicken

- 2 packages (9 ounces each) refrigerated cheese ravioli
- 1 tablespoon olive oil
- ¾ cup matchstick carrots
- ¾ cup thinly sliced celery
- ½ cup chopped onion
- 2 cloves garlic, minced
- 1½ pounds chicken tenders, cut crosswise into halves
- 1 can (about 14 ounces) stewed tomatoes
- ¼ cup dry white wine
- 1 teaspoon dried rosemary
- ¾ teaspoon salt
- ⅛ teaspoon black pepper
- Spinach Pesto (recipe follows)

1. Cook ravioli according to package directions; drain and keep warm.
2. Heat oil in large skillet over medium heat. Add carrots, celery, onion and garlic; cook and stir about 5 minutes or until vegetables are crisp-tender.
3. Add chicken, tomatoes, wine, rosemary, salt and pepper; bring to a boil. Reduce heat to low; simmer, uncovered, about 10 minutes or until chicken is cooked through.
4. Meanwhile prepare Spinach Pesto. Place warm ravioli in serving dish; add pesto and stir gently to coat. Top with chicken and vegetable mixture.

Makes 8 servings

Spinach Pesto

- 2 cups loosely packed fresh spinach
- 2 tablespoons grated Romano cheese
- 2 tablespoons olive oil
- 1 tablespoon lemon juice
- 3 cloves garlic
- 2 teaspoons dried basil
- ¼ teaspoon salt

Combine spinach, cheese, oil, lemon juice, garlic, basil and salt in food processor or blender; process until smooth.

Makes about 1 cup

Fettuccine with Marinara Sauce

- 2 tablespoons olive oil
- 1 medium onion, finely chopped
- 1 small carrot, finely chopped
- 1 small stalk celery, finely chopped
- 2 cloves garlic, finely chopped
- 1 can (28 ounces) peeled plum tomatoes, undrained
- ½ cup water
- ⅓ cup packed chopped fresh basil leaves
- Salt and black pepper
- 1 package (9 ounces) refrigerated fresh fettuccine
- 2 tablespoons butter, thinly sliced
- Grated Parmesan cheese

1. Heat oil in large saucepan over medium heat. Add onion, carrot, celery and garlic; cover and cook about 5 minutes or until onion is golden brown and tender, stirring occasionally.

2. Drain tomatoes, reserving juice. Coarsely crush tomatoes with fingers or wooden spoon. Add tomatoes with juice and water to saucepan; bring to a boil over high heat. Reduce heat to medium-low; simmer, uncovered, about 45 minutes or until sauce is slightly thickened and reduced, stirring frequently. Stir in basil; season with salt and pepper.

3. Meanwhile, cook pasta in large saucepan of salted boiling water according to package directions for al dente. Drain and return to saucepan. Add butter; toss gently to coat. Serve sauce over pasta; sprinkle with cheese.

Makes 4 to 6 servings

Pesto Cavatappi

PESTO

- 2 cups packed fresh basil leaves*
- 1 cup walnuts, toasted**
- ½ cup shredded Parmesan cheese, plus additional for garnish
- 4 cloves garlic
- 1 teaspoon salt
- ¼ teaspoon black pepper
- ¾ cup extra virgin olive oil

**Or substitute 1 cup packed fresh parsley leaves for half of basil.*

***To toast walnuts, cook in medium skillet over medium heat 4 to 5 minutes or lightly browned, stirring frequently.*

PASTA

- 1 package (16 ounces) uncooked cavatappi pasta
- 1 tablespoon extra virgin olive oil
- 2 plum tomatoes, diced (1½ cups)
- 1 package (8 ounces) sliced mushrooms
- ¼ cup dry white wine
- ¼ cup vegetable broth
- ¼ cup whipping cream

1 For pesto, combine basil, walnuts, ½ cup cheese, garlic, salt and pepper in food processor; pulse until coarsely chopped. With motor running, add ¾ cup oil in thin, steady stream; process until well blended. Measure 1 cup pesto for pasta; reserve remaining pesto for another use.

2 Cook pasta in large saucepan of salted boiling water according to package directions for al dente. Drain and return to saucepan; keep warm.

3 Meanwhile, heat 1 tablespoon oil in large skillet over medium-high heat. Add tomatoes and mushrooms; cook about 7 minutes or until most of liquid has evaporated, stirring occasionally. Add wine, broth and cream; bring to a boil. Reduce heat to low; cook about 4 minutes or until sauce has thickened slightly. Stir in 1 cup pesto; cook just until heated through.

4 Pour sauce over pasta; stir gently to coat. Divide pasta among serving bowls; garnish with additional cheese.

Makes 4 to 6 servings

Spaghetti with Roasted Pepper and Tomato Sauce

- **3 red bell peppers**
- **8 ounces uncooked spaghetti**
- **2 tablespoons olive oil**
- **1 medium red onion, finely chopped**
- **1 clove garlic, minced**
- **1 can (about 14 ounces) fire-roasted diced tomatoes**
- **¾ teaspoon salt**
- **¼ teaspoon dried oregano**
- **¼ teaspoon chipotle chile flakes or red pepper flakes**
- **⅛ teaspoon black pepper**
- **½ cup grated Parmesan cheese**

1. Preheat broiler. Place bell peppers on rack in broiler pan; broil 3 to 5 inches from heat source until peppers are blistered and charred on all sides, turning frequently. Transfer to large food storage bag; seal bag and let stand 15 to 20 minutes to loosen skins. Scrape off skins with paring knife. Cut off tops; scrape out and discard seeds. Coarsely chop peppers.
2. Cook pasta according to package directions; drain and keep warm.
3. Meanwhile, heat oil in large skillet over medium-high heat. Add onion and garlic; cook and stir 3 to 5 minutes or until tender. Add roasted peppers; cook and stir 2 minutes.
4. Stir in tomatoes, salt, oregano, chile flakes and black pepper; mix well. Reduce heat to low; simmer 10 minutes. Serve sauce over pasta; sprinkle with cheese.

Makes 4 servings

Farfalle with Shrimp and Broccoli Pesto

- 2 cups broccoli florets
- 2¼ teaspoon salt, divided
- 2 cups uncooked bowtie pasta (farfalle)
- ½ cup loosely packed fresh basil leaves
- 5 tablespoons shredded Parmesan-Romano cheese blend, divided
- 3 tablespoons extra virgin olive oil, divided
- 2 tablespoons chopped walnuts, toasted*
- 2 cloves garlic, crushed, divided
- 6 ounces medium cooked shrimp
- ¼ teaspoon black pepper
- 1 package (6 ounces) baby spinach
- 1 cup halved grape tomatoes

***To toast walnuts, cook in small skillet over medium heat 1 to 2 minutes or lightly browned, stirring frequently.**

1. Bring large saucepan of water to a boil. Add broccoli and 2 teaspoons salt; cook 3 minutes or until tender. Remove to small bowl with slotted spoon; reserve water in saucepan.

2. Cook pasta in reserved water according to package directions for al dente. Drain and return to saucepan; keep warm.

3. Combine broccoli, basil, 3 tablespoons cheese, 2 tablespoons oil, walnuts, 1 clove garlic and remaining ¼ teaspoon salt in food processor or blender; process until smooth. Add to pasta in saucepan; toss gently to coat. Cover to keep warm.

4. Heat remaining 1 tablespoon oil in large skillet over medium heat. Add shrimp, remaining 1 clove garlic and pepper; cook and stir until heated through. Stir in spinach and tomatoes; cook until spinach is wilted and tomatoes begin to soften. Add to pasta; stir gently to combine. Sprinkle with remaining 2 tablespoons cheese.

Makes 4 servings

Chicken and Pasta with Creamy Caper-Herb Sauce

- 6 ounces uncooked egg noodles
- 1 tablespoon olive oil
- 1 pound chicken tenders
- ¼ teaspoon salt
- ¼ teaspoon dried oregano
- ⅓ cup white wine
- ⅓ cup chicken broth
- 4 ounces garlic-and-herb cream cheese
- 3 tablespoons milk
- 3 tablespoons capers, drained and rinsed
- 1 tablespoon grated Parmesan cheese

1. Cook noodles according to package directions; drain and keep warm.
2. Meanwhile, heat oil in large skillet over medium heat. Add chicken; sprinkle with salt and oregano. Cook 5 minutes per side or until chicken is no longer pink in center. Remove to plate.
3. Add wine and broth to skillet; cook 30 seconds, scraping up browned bits from bottom of skillet. Remove from heat; add cream cheese, milk and capers. Stir until cream cheese is melted and sauce is smooth. Return chicken to skillet; cook until heated through.
4. Serve sauce and chicken over noodles; sprinkle with cheese.

Makes 4 servings

Linguine with Clams and Marinara Sauce

- 1⅓ cups Marinara Sauce (recipe follows)
- 8 ounces uncooked linguine
- 1 tablespoon olive oil
- ¼ cup chopped shallots
- 3 cloves garlic, finely chopped
- 2 cans (6 ounces each) minced clams
- 2 tablespoons pesto sauce
- ¼ teaspoon red pepper flakes
- ¼ cup chopped fresh parsley

1. Prepare Marinara Sauce. Cook linguine according to package directions; drain and keep warm.
2. Heat 1 tablespoon oil in large saucepan over medium heat. Add shallots and garlic; cover and cook 2 minutes.
3. Drain clams, reserving ½ cup juice. Add clams, reserved juice, 1½ cups Marinara Sauce, pesto sauce and red pepper flakes to saucepan; cook, uncovered, 10 minutes, stirring occasionally.
4. Pour sauce over linguine; toss to coat. Sprinkle with parsley.

Makes 4 servings

Marinara Sauce

- 1½ tablespoons olive oil
- 3 cloves garlic, minced
- 1 can (28 ounces) Italian plum tomatoes, undrained
- ¼ cup tomato paste
- 2 teaspoons dried basil
- ½ teaspoon sugar
- ½ teaspoon salt
- ¼ teaspoon red pepper flakes

Heat oil in large skillet over medium heat. Add garlic; cook and stir 3 minutes. Stir in tomatoes with juice, tomato paste, basil, sugar, salt and red pepper flakes; bring to a boil. Reduce heat to low; simmer, uncovered, 10 minutes, stirring occasionally.

Makes about 3½ cups

INDEX

INDEX

INDEX

INDEX

Metric Conversion Chart

VOLUME MEASUREMENTS (dry)

1/8 teaspoon = 0.5 mL
1/4 teaspoon = 1 mL
1/2 teaspoon = 2 mL
3/4 teaspoon = 4 mL
1 teaspoon = 5 mL
1 tablespoon = 15 mL
2 tablespoons = 30 mL
1/4 cup = 60 mL
1/3 cup = 75 mL
1/2 cup = 125 mL
2/3 cup = 150 mL
3/4 cup = 175 mL
1 cup = 250 mL
2 cups = 1 pint = 500 mL
3 cups = 750 mL
4 cups = 1 quart = 1 L

VOLUME MEASUREMENTS (fluid)

1 fluid ounce (2 tablespoons) = 30 mL
4 fluid ounces (1/2 cup) = 125 mL
8 fluid ounces (1 cup) = 250 mL
12 fluid ounces (1 1/2 cups) = 375 mL
16 fluid ounces (2 cups) = 500 mL

WEIGHTS (mass)

1/2 ounce = 15 g
1 ounce = 30 g
3 ounces = 90 g
4 ounces = 120 g
8 ounces = 225 g
10 ounces = 285 g
12 ounces = 360 g
16 ounces = 1 pound = 450 g

DIMENSIONS

1/16 inch = 2 mm
1/8 inch = 3 mm
1/4 inch = 6 mm
1/2 inch = 1.5 cm
3/4 inch = 2 cm
1 inch = 2.5 cm

OVEN TEMPERATURES

250°F = 120°C
275°F = 140°C
300°F = 150°C
325°F = 160°C
350°F = 180°C
375°F = 190°C
400°F = 200°C
425°F = 220°C
450°F = 230°C

BAKING PAN SIZES

Utensil	Size in Inches/Quarts	Metric Volume	Size in Centimeters
Baking or Cake Pan (square or rectangular)	8×8×2	2 L	20×20×5
	9×9×2	2.5 L	23×23×5
	12×8×2	3 L	30×20×5
	13×9×2	3.5 L	33×23×5
Loaf Pan	8×4×3	1.5 L	20×10×7
	9×5×3	2 L	23×13×7
Round Layer Cake Pan	8×1½	1.2 L	20×4
	9×1½	1.5 L	23×4
Pie Plate	8×1¼	750 mL	20×3
	9×1¼	1 L	23×3
Baking Dish or Casserole	1 quart	1 L	—
	1½ quart	1.5 L	—
	2 quart	2 L	—